Cambridge Elements ≣

Elements in Publishing and Book Culture
edited by
Samantha Rayner
University College London
Leah Tether
University of Bristol

THE RISE OF AMERICAN GIRLS' LITERATURE

Ashley N. Reese
University of South Florida

CAMBRIDGE
UNIVERSITY PRESS

CAMBRIDGE
UNIVERSITY PRESS

University Printing House, Cambridge CB2 8BS, United Kingdom

One Liberty Plaza, 20th Floor, New York, NY 10006, USA

477 Williamstown Road, Port Melbourne, VIC 3207, Australia

314–321, 3rd Floor, Plot 3, Splendor Forum, Jasola District Centre,
New Delhi – 110025, India

79 Anson Road, #06–04/06, Singapore 079906

Cambridge University Press is part of the University of Cambridge.

It furthers the University's mission by disseminating knowledge in the pursuit of
education, learning, and research at the highest international levels of excellence.

www.cambridge.org
Information on this title: www.cambridge.org/9781108931540
DOI: 10.1017/9781108942546

First published 2021

A catalogue record for this publication is available from the British Library.

ISBN 978-1-108-93154-0 Paperback
ISSN 2514-8524 (online)
ISSN 2514-8516 (print)

The Rise of American Girls' Literature

Elements in Publishing and Book Culture

DOI: 10.1017/9781108942546
First published online: May 2021

Ashley N. Reese
University of South Florida

Author for correspondence: Ashley N. Reese, anreese@usf.edu

ABSTRACT: This Element looks at the publishing history of the genre, girls' literature, in the United States spanning 1850–1940. The genre is set in context, beginning with an examination of the early American women's literature that preceded girls' literature. Then the Element explores several subgenres of girls' literature, the family story, orphan story, school story, as well as African American girls' literature. Underpinning each of these stories is the *bildungsroman*, which overwhelmingly ends with girls "growing down" to marry and raise children, following the ideals outlined in the cult of domesticity.

This Element also has a video abstract: www.cambridge.org/reese

KEYWORDS: *bildungsroman*, domestic realism, women's literature, nineteenth century, twentieth century

ISBNs: 9781108931540 (PB), 9781108942546 (OC)
ISSNs: 2514-8524 (online), 2514-8516 (print)

Contents

1 The Rise of Girls' Literature

Girls' books have a rich publishing tradition in the United States. Beginning in the mid nineteenth century, there is a wide selection of literature about and for girls: from books that are part of the broader American canon, such as Louisa May Alcott's *Little Women*,[1] to the often censored *Forever* (1975) by Judy Blume.[2] How is a mass-market series, for instance, *Sweet Valley High*,[3] similar to the award-winning (although racially problematic) *Little House* books?[4] What does the religious *Elsie Dinsmore* series[5] have in common with Jean Webster's college heroine in *Daddy Long Legs?*[6] With such a vast genre, defining it and understanding its parameters offers a way to not only understand the publishing history of books for girls, but also to interrogate the ideology surrounding girls' literature today. One might say that the future of publishing girls' books lies in the past.

This Element traces the origins of American girls' literature and outlines four major "subgenres" for girls' fiction, which emerged in the mid nineteenth century. While girls' literature, especially so-called "classic" girls' novels, are the center of a few studies, never have girls' texts been examined as an overarching genre in connection with American women's literature. Instead, this important part of children's publishing history has been neglected in favor of examining American children's books as a whole[7] or as part of smaller subgenres, including North American orphan girls' novels,[8] or "classic" Anglo-American girls' books,[9] without defining the genre parameters. One

---

[1] L. M. Alcott, *Little Women* (Boston, MA: Roberts Brothers, 1868–9).

[2] J. Blume, *Forever* (New York: Bradbury Press, 1975).

[3] F. Pascal, *Sweet Valley High* series (New York: Random House, 1983–2003).

[4] L. I. Wilder, *Little House* series (New York: Harper & Brothers, 1932–71).

[5] M. Finley, *Elsie Dinsmore* series (New York: M.W. Dodd, 1867–1905).

[6] J. Webster, *Daddy Long Legs* (New York: The Century Company, 1912).

[7] See A. S. MacLeod, *American Childhood: Essays on Children's Literature of the Nineteenth and Twentieth Centuries* (Athens, GA: University of Georgia Press, 1994).

[8] See J. S. Sanders, *Disciplining Girls: Understanding the Origins of the Classic Orphan Girl Story* (Baltimore: Johns Hopkins University Press, 2011).

[9] See S. Foster & J. Simons, *What Katy Read: Feminist Re-Readings of 'Classic' Stories for Girls* (Iowa City: University of Iowa Press, 1995).

of the foundational works on broader American publishing history, John Tebbel's *A History of Book Publishing in the United States*, gets numerous facts wrong about girls' texts, for example, accrediting *Little Women*'s illustrations to Louisa Alcott, instead of to her sister, May, and conflating its publication date with the text's sequel in 1869.[10]

Girls' literature is vaster than the "classic" novels that frequently are included in literary history, books such as Susan Coolidge's *What Katy Did* (1872)[11] and Eleanor Porter's *Pollyanna* (1913).[12] Lesser-known texts influenced their contemporary market and paved the way for this major branch of children's publishing. Although few may now read Annie Fellows Johnston's *Little Colonel* series (1895–1912)[13] or Lela Horn Richards' *Caroline* series (1921–1923),[14] these texts used to be in conversation with the so-called classics. Together, they form a better understanding of what girls' literature has been and what it is today. Although only a handful of female authors remain in the public consciousness, in actuality, in the second half of the nineteenth century, there was a "rise of women to prominence as authors, mostly fiction, a trend which was only beginning."[15] Before 1800, only four women had published works in the United States; by 1872, "nearly three-fourths of the novels written that year in America came from their pens."[16] Many of their works were written for children, and, of these, many were specifically about and for girls.

Most of these books were authored by white women. As Lynn S. Cockett and Janet R. Kleinberg note, emerging American children's literature in the nineteenth century was "not truly democratic in its

---

[10] J. Tebbel, *A History of Book Publishing, Vol. II: The Expansion of an Industry, 1865–1919* (New York: R.R. Bowker, 1975), p. 598.

[11] S. Coolidge, *What Katy Did* (Boston, MA: Roberts Brothers, 1872).

[12] E. H. Porter, *Pollyanna* (Boston, MA: L.C. Page, 1913).

[13] A. F. Johnston, *Little Colonel* series (Boston, MA: L.C. Page, 1895–1912).

[14] L. H. Richards, *Caroline* series (Boston, MA: Little, Brown, 1921–23).

[15] J. Tebbel, *A History of Book Publishing in the United States, Vol. I: The Creation of an Industry, 1630–1865* (New York: R.R. Bowker, 1972), p. 543.

[16] Ibid.

representation."[17] This tendency persists in children's book publishing, with a recent study showing that Black authors wrote 5.26 percent of children's books published in the United States in 2019; for comparison, only 21.05 percent total were written by authors of color.[18] Frequently, critics, by omission or indeed direct design, publish histories that only consider books about white children. However, the white, middle-class girls' story is not a complete picture of the publishing market at this time, neither is it an accurate picture of America. While the number of books is not as plentiful, the publishing history of African American girls' literature gives a better picture of American girls' literature. In an effort to broaden our understanding of girls' novels, this Element seeks to include these books. I must note the problematic use of African American girls' literature as a label, as it further affirms the standardized "girls' literature" as necessarily white while "Othering" the non-white protagonist and/or reader. I do not claim to know the answer to this troubling division, but my hope is that by including the ways in which African American girls' literature fits into the broader genre we might continue to include more voices in our understanding of girls' literature and its publication history.

As the nineteenth century progressed, book publishing became more prominent in the United States, due in part to the rise of the middle class and its purchasing power. Around this time, childhood became a delimited and celebrated period.[19] As a result of these two intersecting events, books of pleasure, not just of instruction, practically burst onto the market, and, among them, fiction specifically for girls emerged. These books are often part of a series. Although some early American girls' literature, such as *The*

---

[17] L. S. Cockett and J. R. Kleinberg, "Periodical Literature for African-American Young Adults: A Neglected Resource" in K.P. Smith (ed.), *African-American Voices in Young Adult Literature: Tradition, Transition, Transformation* (Latham, MD: Scarecrow Press, 1994), pp. 115–67, 118.

[18] Cooperative Children's Book Center, Books by and/or about Black, Indigenous, and People of Color (2020). https://ccbc.education.wisc.edu/literature-resources/ccbc-diversity-statistics/books-by-and-or-about-poc-2019/.

[19] G. Avery, *Behold the Child: American Children and their Books 1621–1922* (London: Bodley Head, 1994), p. 122.

Wide, Wide World (1850), are standalone texts, the majority of the books that follow, including *Elsie Dinsmore* (1867) and *Little Women* (1868), are the first in a series. Turning a successful book into a series – whether comprised of twenty-eight books, like *Elsie*, or four books, like *Little Women* – clearly appeals to publishers. Readers already know the characters and are more likely to continue to buy books in an established series, minimizing both production risks and cost. Advertisements in magazines including *The Youth's Companion* and *The Bookman* focus on the appeal of "established juveniles" for the "many little girls who have already made friends with" the series' heroine.[20] These advertisements promote the newest book alongside its predecessors, potentially drawing the attention of new and established readers of the series, making it known those books that readers might have "missed." This publishing trend of relying on readers' invested interest in series fiction continues today, with mass market paperback series, such as *Sweet Valley High*.

Gendered book marketing is found in early twentieth-century periodical advertisements. In the nineteenth century, advertisements for children's books were often classified under the broader category of "juvenile literature." In a 1909 notice of recently published girls' books, the difference between boys' and girls' books is outlined. The notice acknowledges the quality of girls' literature, while simultaneously observing the superiority of the *content* of boys' books, namely, "a series of adventures which tend to keep up the interest."[21] The notice then outlines almost verbatim the girls' subgenres explored in this Element: "a story of school or home life or of the girl's effort to make her way in the world in the face of adverse circumstance."[22] (I would argue that the expression "adverse circumstances" describes the orphan girl's story.) Although perhaps reductive, the 1909 notice observes that fictional heroes have adventures, while heroines are limited by their setting. A girls' escapade at home is inevitably tamer than a boys' escapade at sea. Marketing books based on gender remains popular to this day.

---

[20] "Advertisement 151," *The Bookman: A Review of Books and Life*, 30.6 (1910), p. 822.
[21] "Real books for real girls," *New York Times* (5 Dec. 1909), p. LS20. [22] Ibid.

Using the Library of Congress's catalog, the copyright book depository in the United States,[23] we can start to trace the publishing history of girls' literature. A search of "juvenile fiction" in the Library of Congress's catalog results in well-over 10,000 titles published between 1850 and 1940, the years examined in this Element. Observing select years can provide a better idea of the publication of both girls' and children's literature and the relationship between the two. To conduct this search, I looked for books that are classified as PZ7, the Library of Congress's classification for juvenile fiction, that are in English, are identified as a book, and were published in the specified timeframe. Although I narrowed the search to books published in the United States, the corpus was not limited to American books, as American publishers distributed works by non-American authors. This search provided the number of general children's literature shown in Figure 1. To identify girls' literature was a little more haphazard, as not all the books are digitized or even summarized online, thus, I was reliant on the metadata to determine whether the title might be girls' literature. If the title referenced a girl and was by a female author, unless I knew otherwise,[24] I included it in my count of girls' literature. This methodology seeks to "understanding trends with time."[25] The data gathered is not foolproof, as "even published government figures are not necessarily clear or reliable."[26] Still, the graph in Figure 1 gives a sense of publishing history of both children's and girls' literature in the United States.

As noted in this chart, the number of children's books published in the United States steadily increased throughout the period this Element examines. Publication of girls' literature does not increase at the same rate, but remains fairly consistent: in 1870, it comprises 27.8 percent of the children's books; in

[23] The Library of Congress became the centralized copyright depository for the United States in 1870. Previously, copyright texts were held by clerks of court.

[24] For example, I excluded the *Aunt Jane's Nieces* series, as Edith Van Dyne is a pseudonym of L. Frank Baum.

[25] A. Weedon, "The Uses of Quantification" in S. Eliot and J. Rose (eds.), *A Companion to the History of the Book*, 2nd ed. (Hoboken, NJ: John Wiley & Sons, 2019), pp. 31–50, 40.

[26] Ibid., p. 38.

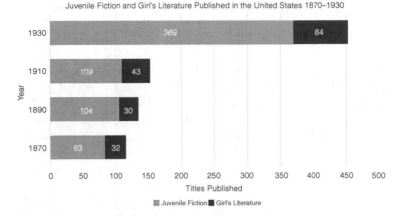

Figure 1 A graph of juvenile fiction and girls' literature published in the United States

1890, it is 22.4 percent; in 1910, it is the highest percentage at 28.3 percent; and, in 1930, which also includes the greatest number and variety of children's books, it falls to 18.5 percent. As these numbers indicate, girls' literature is a prominent part of children's literature. To neglect this genre would be to skew our scholarly understanding of juvenile American literature.

1.1 Defining American Girls' Literature

Girls' literature can be defined as a book written about a girl, for a girl reader,[27] with the targeted audience identified in its name, similar to children's or young adult literature. Of course, implied readership is not always translated into actual readers: boys and girls, adults and children alike read these books. For the purpose of this Element, the authors are women, mirroring other girls' literature studies.[28] However, in identifying

---

[27] D. Sardella-Ayres and A. N. Reese, "Constructing girls' literature through the *bildungsroman* in Canada and the United States," *Girlhood Studies: An Interdisciplinary Journal*, 13.1 (2020), 33–49, 34.

[28] Cf. ibid.

those stipulations, not only are we led to ask *who* these girls and women are, but as a result *what* the books reveal about them. To ask these questions is to engage Judith Butler's groundbreaking argument that gender is "a becoming, and constructing," with gender reflected as "a set of repeated acts within a highly rigid regulatory frame."[29] Girls' literature offers a particular expectation for womanhood. As Elaine Showalter observes, a "girls' story" is "designed to bridge a gap between the schoolroom and the drawing room, to recommend docility, marriage, and obedience rather than autonomy or adventure."[30] Consequently, these nineteenth- and early twentieth-century novels collectively imagine a single ending for heroines (and arguably, their readers).

The female *bildungsroman*, or coming-of-age story, underpins the genre of girls' literature: "[T]he heroine's trajectory of growth and development remains analogous for both girls' fiction and girls' *bildungsromane*, despite some texts ending before the heroine reaches adulthood. The socialization of the heroine into the roles of wife and mother remains central to girls' literature."[31] Indeed, whether the heroine begins the story as a tomboy or a college student,[32] her ending usually culminates in matrimony. Whereas, in Showalter's terms, a male *bildungsroman* features a boy going on an "adventure," acquiring the "autonomy"[33] that is central to his adulthood; a female *bildungsroman*, however, is about community integration. More specifically, the girl becomes a caretaker of others and a home, preparing for marriage and motherhood. In losing her individuality, Annis Pratt argues that instead of "growing up," the girl "grow[s] down."[34] These restrictions often are increased exponentially when the heroine is African American.

---

[29] J. Butler, *Gender Trouble* (New York: Routledge, 1990), p. 45.

[30] E. Showalter, *Sister's Choice: Tradition and Change in American Women's Writing* (Oxford: Oxford University Press, 1991), p. 50.

[31] Sardella-Ayres and Reese, "Where to from here?," 34.

[32] See M. A. Abate, *Tomboys: A Literary and Cultural History* (Philadelphia: Temple University Press, 2008).

[33] Showalter, *Sister's Choice*, p. 50.

[34] A. Pratt, *Archetypal Patterns in Women's Fiction* (Bloomington: Indiana University Press, 1981), p. 30.

These developmental ideas are based on the period's clear distinctions between girls and boys. Barbara Welter observes that "[t]he nineteenth century was confident that it knew the differences between the sexes and that these differences were total and innate."[35] Specifically: "Women were inherently more religious, modest, passive, submissive and domestic than men."[36] These ascribed qualities fit the domestic role assigned to girls. Thus, an American adolescent was meant to help her mother run the household, practicing the virtues that supposedly are central to womanhood. As the twentieth century dawned and women attended higher education, more opportunities were made available in girlhood. However, the restrictions for women remained the same, making the gap between girlhood and womanhood that much more pronounced.

Betty Friedan's seminal, albeit problematic, *The Feminine Mystique*,[37] followed two decades after the girls' literature examined in this Element. Her "problem that has no name," namely, women's "dissatisfaction" and "yearning" for a life beyond domestic duties,[38] helped usher in second-wave feminism. My critique put forth in this Element follows Friedan's claims; namely, that women should be able to choose the life they want. Friedan observes, "experts [tell] women their role [is] to seek fulfillment as wives and mothers";[39] indeed, this message is central to girls' literature. While Friedan's critique might be too modern to bear significant weight in reading earlier values, women petitioned for equality concurrent with these texts. First-wave feminism led to the Nineteenth Amendment in 1919, granting voting rights to American white women. Nevertheless, these girls' texts almost never mention suffrage,[40] and a career, if entertained, occurs before marriage. Instead, there is typically one path for heroines. As Nancy Rosoff and Stephanie Spencer observe, for authors of adolescent girls' fiction: "[T]heir presentation of femininity both teaches the reader

---

[35] B. Welter, *Dimity Convictions: The American Woman in the Nineteenth Century* (Athens: Ohio University Press, 1976), p. 4.

[36] Ibid. [37] B. Friedan, *The Feminine Mystique* (New York: W.W. Norton, 1963).

[38] Ibid., p. 15. [39] Ibid.

[40] The only text I found that mentions women's suffrage is Jean Webb's *Daddy Long Legs* (1912).

how they *should* behave *and* reflects their contemporary society's expectations of what is 'natural' female behavior."[41] Unsurprisingly, many girls' books preserve a socially conservative view of acceptable feminine behavior, as they had to meet the approval of the generally male-run publishing houses, as well as that of the social gatekeepers, librarians, bookshop owners, and parents.

While studies of children's books, such as Gillian Avery's *Behold the Child* (1994), often center only on American books, studies on girls' literature rarely make such a distinction, instead grouping together English-speaking texts, whether that means Anglo-American (see Shirley Foster and Judy Simons' 1995 *What Katy Read*) or English-speaking North American (see Joe Sutliff Sanders' 2011 *Disciplining Girls*). These American girls' books did not exist and, indeed, were not read in isolation. The borders between Anglophone readers were often blurred with Canadian books published out of New England and British books imported to the American market. While this Element focuses solely on American girls' literature, it is with the acknowledgment that these books (and their readers) were in conversation with girls' books printed in the United Kingdom, Canada, and other English-speaking nations. Indeed, girls' literature broadly shares similarities, such as female authorship, readership, and protagonist, but some qualities are culturally specific. American girls' books emphasize representing a new nation, everexpanding opportunities, and deliberately differentiating oneself from Britain. These ideas take root in the American women's fiction examined in section 2 and remain central to the girls' fiction that follows.

Perhaps the strongest example of patriotism is Lela Horn Richards' *Then Came Caroline* (1921),[42] in which the eponymous protagonist moves west with her family. Caroline quickly adapts to this environment, where social class is less important, mirroring the supposed equality of the United States. Similarly, Caroline's gaze remains fixed on the Rocky Mountains, which symbolize Caroline's future, as she dreams of living beyond them. Thus,

---

[41] N. G. Rosoff and S. Spencer, *British and American School Stories, 1910–1960: Fiction, Femininity, and Friendship* (Cham, Switzerland: Palgrave Macmillan, 2019), p. 16; emphasis in original.

[42] L. H. Richards, *Then Came Caroline* (Boston, MA: Little, Brown, 1921).

when a relative offers Caroline the opportunity to move to England, Caroline's response has to be "no," in order to preserve her American identity and continue her journey westward, mirroring the nation's growth, as well as the pioneering spirit attributed to the American manifest destiny.

Similarly, American identity is a theme in Susan Warner's *The Wide, Wide World* (1850).[43] When the heroine, Ellen, is sent to live in Scotland, her aunt, Lady Keith, asks her to relinquish her American citizenship. Ellen refuses, declaring: "I had a great deal rather be an American."[44] Ellen's devotion to the United States stands almost in defiance to Great Britain and its classicism invoked by her aunt's title. Ellen's push for equality can be seen in her knowledge-based patriotism: she reads biographies of George Washington and debates her uncle on the justification of the American Revolution. Both Warner and Richards' texts point to the importance of heroines' American pride, which, in part, is defined as not British.

Not all the texts are as explicit in their patriotism as these novels, although heroines are usually proud to be American. Women's patriotic contributions were in raising sons to thereby indirectly influence the nation's development.[45] While this theme is echoed in British girls' books, the overtness of the patriotism in American girls' books, including the supposed lack of classicism, runs contrary to British girls' texts. Thus, the novels included here are part of a socially conservative book history, wherein the ideology is practically uniform: girls, no matter how autonomous at the beginning of the novel or series, are willing, even happy, to give up this freedom for marriage and motherhood. A model of potential subversion is constructed only to have this subversion contained at the end. This trajectory underpins the genre of girls' literature.

1.2 Corpus Novels

This Element traces the development of American girls' literature in the time period 1850–1940. In order to have a clear focus, the texts chosen are

---

[43] S. Warner, *The Wide, Wide World* (New York: G.P. Putnam, 1850).

[44] Ibid., p. 499.

[45] G. Matthews, *"Just a Housewife": The Rise and Fall of Domesticity in America* (Oxford: Oxford University Press, 1987), p. 35.

"realistic" fiction and were published in book form at some point, sometimes following serialization. All of these texts have female authors. The number of girls' books published in this span are too vast to be covered in detail. However, I have included texts that are still in print, as well as lesser-known books to try to show the range of girls' literature. Each section features four to ten novels, in an attempt to uncover the publishing standards for that book type. To locate texts, I utilized *The Girls' Series Companion: 1997*,[46] which supplied brief summaries of girls' series fiction titles beginning in the nineteenth century. Although its focus is series fiction, this resource helped me identify lesser-known books that fit the subgenres examined in this Element, particularly as the metadata in Special Collections libraries often lack plot summaries. From there, I worked with Special Collections librarian, Suzan Alteri, to expand my search to include African American girls' literature, which, typically, were not series. For each section, I have included in-print and out-of-print books. In depending on universities' special collections and digitized texts for out-of-print texts, there is an acknowledgment that curation does not preserve every book. No collection is ideologically neutral, and so the very books that might have challenged the boundaries of girls' literature could be the ones that were not preserved.

The timeframe chosen follows what Reese and Sardella-Ayres[47] argue is the standard time period for classic girls' literature, with the invention of the "teenager" after World War II disrupting the coming-of-age stories typical of the earlier period (and ushering in the "young adult" genre). The majority of the heroines examined in this Element are what we might identify today as adolescents. This concept was just emerging in the United States in the last decades of the nineteenth century, "marked on the one hand by [a girl's] first menstruation at fourteen or fifteen, and on the other by her marriage at eighteen to twenty."[48] These ages are more guidelines than hard boundaries, and Welter notes the "significance" of the "twentieth birthday" as when girls

---

[46] The Society of Phantom Friends. *The Girls' Series Companion: 1997* (Henderson, NV: SynSine Press, 1997).

[47] Sardella-Ayres and Reese, "Where to from here?," 34.

[48] Welter, *Dimity Convictions*, p. 3.

"abandoned the lightheartedness of girlhood and prepared for the weighty cares of domesticity and maternity."[49] As a result, the fiction published reflects this concept, with stories that reflect this period in a girl's life. Although the terms "girls" and "girlhood" have diminutive connotations in modern society, the novels use these terms and, thus, so does this Element.

Beginning with locating its publishing roots in American women's literature, the second section draws similarities between mid nineteenth-century women's novels and the girls' novels that follow. The Element then examines three distinct subgenres of girls' literature, namely, family, orphan, and schoolgirls' literature, noting the protagonists' agency, but also the often-conservative expectations of fictional girls in society. Section 6 focuses on African American girls' literature, drawing comparisons between the three subgenres of mainstream girls' literature from this time, but also noting the differences given the limited social opportunities available to women of color at the turn of the century. By exploring these different types of American girls' literature, I offer a better understanding of the socially conservative character arc for girls, which reflects the culture in which these books are being written, published, and read. As a result, this Element extends previous research with the aim of disrupting this single ending in future publishing endeavors, purposefully offering options in addition to or apart from the expectation of marriage and motherhood in a girl's future.

---

[49] Ibid.

2 "Thus Shall the Star of Domestic Peace Arise": Early American Women's Literature

As the nineteenth century dawned, women's novels grappled with the female role in the newly formed United States. Subsequently, there is a distinct shift in American women's literature published between the end of the eighteenth century and the beginning of the nineteenth. These early novels, such as Susanna Rowson's *Charlotte Temple* (1794),[50] feature heroines seduced by men and thus fated to die. However, by the 1820s, these character types become minor characters. In this shift, the home as a microcosm for the country becomes central to women's literature. Authors such as Catharine Maria Sedgwick[51] led the way, writing about domestic life in New England. Their focus on family echoes the cultural idea that a burgeoning nation depends on women: raising their children, particularly sons, influences the future, and caring for their husbands helps form the country in the present. As Glenna Matthews observes: "The cult of domesticity was predicated in part on the idea that the home has an expressly political function."[52] In embodying this belief, American heroines set an example for female readers.

In this way, the patriarchal culture of the early United States crafted an idealistic female role. Here confining women to the home was necessary to better the country, but the reality was women had little direct power. What nineteenth-century publications called the "cult of true womanhood" "could be divided into four cardinal virtues – piety, purity, submissiveness and domesticity."[53] These four virtues center on a spiritual demureness, as women embody the angelic heart of the house. As pervasive as these ideas were, unsurprisingly, they are present and even celebrated in the following novels. At the heart of this femininity is honoring women's domestic roles: mother and wife, housekeeper and caretaker. Girlhood and its experiences, including education and travel, are intended to prepare girls for these future tasks. In this way, these texts are "novels of education": they encourage self-

---

[50] S. Rowson, *Charlotte Temple* (Philadelphia: Matthew Carey, 1794).

[51] C. M. Sedgwick, *A New-England Tale* (New York: Bliss & White, 1822).

[52] Matthews, *"Just a Housewife,"* p. 35.   [53] Welter, *Dimity Convictions*, p. 21.

discipline in "forward[ing] the development, in young, female readers, of a specific kind of character."[54] Although the individual is often valued alongside the collective in women's fiction,[55] heroines must still lovingly perform their duty, which is typified as raising children and supporting their husbands. Notably however, not all female characters are presumed to be "formed for domestic content,"[56] and several novels, as we shall see, depict women choosing to remain unmarried. They enter what Maglina Lubovich terms a "republican marriage,"[57] wherein they help raise the children in their community. In this manner, these early women's novels are more progressive than the girls' fiction that follows. The values may remain the same, but the ways those values manifest are allowed to differ in women's literature.

In the early nineteenth century, publishing novels was a risky venture, so in spite of the rise in women authors, they were more likely to publish short stories in magazines and annuals.[58] Thus, these four novels, published between 1822 and 1844, are anomalies. These books are bound with either sheepskin (a cheap alternative to leather) or cloth. The titles are printed on the spines; gilt lettering is used for the cloth-bound books. There are no illustrations for these four texts, although the 1844 novel has decorative blind stamping on its cloth cover. Each book examined in this section is one volume, around 300 pages long, although longer texts were sometimes published in two volumes.

Importantly, these novels were published in the United States, further emphasizing the American identity highlighted in the narratives. There are four separate publishers for these texts – Bliss & White; Harper & Brothers; Hilliard, Grey; and T.H. Carter – showing no clear pattern as to who was publishing women's literature. Advertisements look different than those in the latter half of the nineteenth century. Several booksellers listed these titles as in stock; similarly, monthly literary reviews share new

[54] N. Baym, *Woman's Fiction: A Guide to Novels by and about Women in America, 1820–1870*, 2nd ed. (Ithaca, NY: Cornell University Press, 1993), p. xix.

[55] Ibid., p. xx. [56] Ibid., p. xxvi.

[57] M. Lubovich, "'Married or single?': Catharine Maria Sedgwick on old maids, wives, and marriage," *Legacy*, 25.1 (2008), 23–40, 25.

[58] Baym, *Woman's Fiction*, p. 63.

releases grouped by publisher. Overall, the information is reduced to title, author, publisher, and, occasionally, price. One example of more detail comes in a 1844 monthly literary bulletin, which describes A.J. Graves' *Girlhood and Womanhood; or Sketches of my Schoolmates* (1844)[59] as "intended to show the effects of a right training of the mind. The pictures are drawn from human nature, and exhibit varieties of female character."[60] This account focuses on the novel's realism, as well as the lessons the novel contains. Graves' name is not mentioned; instead, she is listed as the author of "Woman in America," presumably to appeal to readers of the earlier work. These books are listed by location of publisher: either the United States or England, further emphasizing the Americanness of these books. Amid the "varieties of female character" eschewed by the advertisement, each text centers around an idealized heroine, one who reveres the tenets of marriage and motherhood, even when she remains unmarried. In this way, these texts collectively denote the kind of woman needed to form a new nation.

2.1 Improving Motherhood

With such a strong cultural emphasis on motherhood, these novels often focus on the separation between a mother and child, for in early women's literature, "home and mother are the secular counterpart to heaven and God."[61] For this reason, many of the novels begin with the heroine losing one or both of her parents, being removed from friends, or sent away from home. The novel ends once the heroine has created her own family, restoring "heaven-on-earth" by becoming a mother herself.

Jane Elton in Sedgwick's *A New-England Tale* (1822) is described as "an angel upon earth,"[62] and, duly, Jane overcomes her parents' poor examples.

---

[59] A. J. Graves, *Girlhood and Womanhood; or, Sketches of my Schoolmates* (Boston, MA: T.H. Carter, 1844).

[60] "Monthly literary bulletin," *The United States Magazine, and Democratic Review*, 14.4 (1844), 552.

[61] M. Noble, *Masochistic Pleasures of Sentimental Literature* (Princeton, NJ: Princeton University Press, 2000), p. 67.

[62] Sedgwick, *A New-England Tale*, p. 116.

Before his death, Mr. Elton accumulated debts, in part, because Mrs. Elton never intervened. Although Mrs. Elton's "habitual passiveness"[63] might be viewed as consistent with the cult of domesticity, the novel critiques her behavior. In order to build a new nation, the novel argues, wives must be active helpmates to their husbands. Jane demonstrates that she possesses this fiscal responsibility. When Jane's parents die, she must bear their debt. Jane uses her earned money to pay her father's debt, holding herself accountable for her father's behavior in a way her mother never did. In this action, Jane atones for her mother's inaction, while asserting her ability to partner her future husband.

On her parents' deaths, Jane comes to live with her Aunt Wilson, a hypocritical Christian widow who acts out of duty, rather than love. Although women's novels typically hold duty in high regard, it must be rooted in what Nina Baym terms "social love."[64] This emphasis aligns with Lubovich's "republican marriage," in which family and community unite for the "civic responsibility and duty that come with raising future citizens."[65] In this light, when Jane is orphaned, her community, particularly her aunt, should have welcomed her. There is little republican goodwill in Aunt Wilson's adoption; rather, she acts out of fear of her neighbors' condemnation. Aunt Wilson is cruel to Jane and indulgent with her immoral children. Aunt Wilson is thus a foil for the mother Jane will become. Even before her marriage, Jane has proved her mothering abilities by participating in republican marriage. At the novel's end, Jane marries Mr. Lloyd and moves into her childhood home, what Marianne Noble calls "secular . . . heaven."[66] Jane now claims the roles of capable mother and wife, replacing her flawed mother figures and asserting her place in the cult of domesticity.

While the text does not directly relate motherhood to forming a new nation, in the preface, Sedgwick frames the novel in terms of "sketches of the character and manners of our own country."[67] The title, *A New-England Tale*, implies that the story is indicative of life in the northern United States,

---

[63] Ibid., p. 15.   [64] Baym, *Woman's Fiction*, p. 25.

[65] Lubovich, "Married or single?," p. 25.   [66] Noble, *Masochistic Pleasures*, p. 67.

[67] Sedgwick, *New-England Tale*, p. vii.

and although a work of fiction, it argues that a noble American woman is a helpmate to one's husband and a mother to all children.

The maternal separation takes a different form in Caroline Gilman's *Recollections of a Southern Matron* (1838).[68] When Cornelia Wilton describes her mother, it is as someone managing a household; rarely, if ever, is she portrayed as a loving mother or wife. Instead, she is "charm[ing]"[69] and socially capable. One chapter describes Mrs. Wilton's failed attempt to teach her children; she is too busy tending to the needs of the plantation to adequately instruct them. Instead, the enslaved women "mother" the children. One such caretaker sacrifices her life for Cornelia's youngest sister, aligning her more closely with the idealized mother.

Cornelia's moral and religious example in the novel is not her mother, but her male tutor, Charles Duncan. To have an unrelated male character as a moral guide is unusual in both women's and girls' literature; however, because of his illness and eventual death, he poses no sexual threat. Instead, Charles becomes her somewhat feminized mother figure, sharing his Christian beliefs and strict moral code with her. His guidance remains influential, as she often recalls "his rich monitions, his practical excellence."[70] When he dies, their separation becomes the heart of the novel, much as Jane's mother's death is central to *A New-England Tale*. Indeed, Cornelia seeks to find a husband of whom Charles would have approved. Charles, not her mother, is Cornelia's model for goodness.

Motherhood rather than wifehood becomes the focus of Cornelia's adult home. Cornelia's marriage moves from one of sentiment to one of working as a helpmate, a progression that the novel presents as "natural" and "sensible."[71] What Amy McCandless terms their "inegalitarian marriage,"[72] divides into separate spheres, whereupon Cornelia's husband is frequently absent and Cornelia assumes the role of household manager that her mother held. Cornelia warns the reader: "Let [a husband] know nothing of the

[68] C. Gilman, *Recollections of a Southern Matron* (New York: Harper & Brothers, 1838).

[69] Gilman, *Southern Matron*, p. 24. [70] Ibid., p. 215. [71] Ibid., p. 257.

[72] A. T. McCandless, "Concepts of patriarchy in popular novels of antebellum southern women," *Studies in Popular Culture*, 10.2 (1987), 1–16, 11.

struggle . . . thus shall the star of domestic peace arise."[73] Accordingly, the wife's role is to acquiesce to her husband's lifestyle, partnering with him in a way that recalls *A New-England Tale*.

Motherhood, in contrast, is presented in idealized terms. Cornelia describes her relationship with her son as all consuming: "I thought, as is the case with most American mothers, of little else but him."[74] This mother–child bond stands in sharp contrast to her mother's example: Cornelia would never prioritize the household over her children. Motherhood is also central to Cornelia's religious identity. Her faith is strengthened by her children's deaths, which leave her committed "to fulfil the command of Jesus."[75] This deeper understanding of religious duty reiterates the mother–child bond as a secular counterpart to Christianity. Cornelia's mothering also is tied to her patriotic identity. Despite the title's use of "southern," Cornelia prioritizes her American identity over a regional one, common for the time.[76] The rift she observes is with those outside the United States: unlike "foreign travellers [*sic*]," the American "mother seek[s] her dearest charm at home" with her child.[77] Thus, to be an American woman is to stay home raising a new generation. As with Jane Elton, we might view Cornelia as an improvement of her mother, as she follows her tutor's moral teachings and assumes a sentimental motherhood.

2.2 Flawed and Flawless Heroines

Motherhood, although frequently present even in its absence, is not always central to the protagonist's *bildungsroman* in early American women's literature. Sometimes the focus shifts to the type of woman one should become (presumably in order to be a better mother). To accomplish this lesson, often "counterpoint" heroines are present, one "flawless and the [other] flawed."[78] While the flawless heroine lives a near-perfect life, the flawed heroine suffers, illustrating the author's "strenuous insistence that such trials, because they called out otherwise dormant abilities, could

---

[73] Gilman, *Southern Matron*, p. 257.   [74] Ibid., p. 264.   [75] Ibid., p. 268.

[76] N. Baym, *Feminism and American Literary History* (New Brunswick, NJ: Rutgers University Press, 1992), p. 190.

[77] Gilman, *Southern Matron*, p. 110.   [78] Baym, *Woman's Fiction*, p. 35.

become occasions for 'perfecting' the character."[79] Two novels in particular utilize these heroine types as a means of teaching readers how to become better women.

Eliza Lee Cabot Follen's 1838 *Sketches of Married Life*[80] depicts two young women's courtships and subsequent marriages. Amy is a devout Christian; her foil, Fanny, is not as morally inclined and, thus, suffers through much of the novel. Through hardships of her own creation, Fanny must learn to become the ideal woman Amy already is. Fanny and Amy have different opinions of marriage. Fanny argues a woman is implicitly powerless in marriage, as she relinquishes her name, property, and even freewill. However, Amy is convinced "there can be no slavish submission, where true love exists."[81] In spite of her misgivings, Fanny enters a marriage of subservience. Fanny insists on obeying her husband, acting on her perception of what he wants, even as it leads to her unhappiness. When Fanny almost dies, the two resolve to change, resulting in a happy marriage. Amy and her husband never need to learn such a lesson. The novel ends observing: "Amy was [her husband's] intimate adviser and efficient helpmate, his equal partner, his best friend."[82] Arguably, Amy's marriage of so-called equal partnership is more socially advanced than modern readers might expect.

Marriage is the focus of Follen's text, with few references to motherhood, distinguishing this text from *New-England Tale* and *Southern Matron*. *Married Life* still asserts separate spheres in marriage; Amy acknowledges: "I can not help him transact his business at the counting-room, neither can he assist me in my household affairs; but whenever, and in whatever way, we can be mutually interested and occupied, we shall act together."[83] Thus, Amy's expertise supposedly is rooted in the domestic, her husband's in business. Neither Amy nor Fanny works outside of home, although Amy supports a charity school. While their financial situations vary, both women consistently have at least one servant helping with domestic tasks. Here,

---

[79] Ibid., p. 36.

[80] E. L. C. Follen, *Sketches of Married Life* (Boston, MA: Hilliard, Gray, & Co., 1838).

[81] Ibid., p. 32.   [82] Ibid., p. 304.   [83] Ibid., p. 176.

marriage can offer a sort of freedom, where a woman's voice is valued, as long as the domestic boundaries of marriage and motherhood (and the privilege of social class) are intact.

The flawed and flawless heroines are present in Graves' 1844 *Girlhood and Womanhood*. The novel examines the lives of ten girls through their former classmate's narration. All eleven girls attended a boarding school run by Mrs. Norville, whose guidance is rooted in Christian precepts. As was common for early American women's seminaries,[84] her teachings focus on domesticity: "It was her endeavor to prepare her scholars . . . to become good wives, mothers and mistresses of families."[85] On leaving school, most do not enter angelic womanhood; instead, we learn of girls who flirted, were tempted by wealth, or married hastily. Like Follen's flawed Fanny, each imperfect woman's sufferings redeem her, causing her to embrace the cult of domesticity.

There are two characters who are held up as what Baym terms "flaw-less." The first is angelic Sarah Sherman, who honors her domestic duties in her pursuit of education. She suffers when her husband begins to accumulate debt. In the flawed and flawless dichotomy, a flawless heroine, with no lesson to learn, should not suffer. However, Sarah's financial influence is more limited than previous heroines'. Sarah endeavors "to please her husband,"[86] but like Cornelia in *Southern Matron*, they are not equal. Sarah's suffering ends only when her husband gains wealth; *he* learns no lesson because the fictional flawed husband is not expected to change. Sarah's story appears to warn readers that even flawless women are at the mercy of their husbands.

The second flawless character, the narrator Ellen Maitland, represents the merit of not marrying. According to the novel, American women are allotted an unusual degree of agency. Instead of "parental restriction over young females until they are given up to the guardianship of husbands,"[87] American women have freedom as illustrated by Ellen. She remains unwed, in what she repeatedly calls "single blessedness."[88] Ellen echoes the novel's sentiment: "There is to me no sweeter picture in the world than a domestic

---

[84] Welter, *Dimity Convictions*, p. 23. [85] Graves, *Girlhood and Womanhood*, p. 10. [86] Ibid., p. 197. [87] Ibid., p. 38. [88] Ibid., p. 208.

hearth with its devoted father, its fond, thoughtful mother, and the little clustering band of lovely, affectionate children."[89] Ellen values domesticity and so enters a republican marriage by helping care for her adopted brother's children. Ellen avoids Sarah's fate and participates in motherhood, which these texts universally laud. Thus, *Girlhood and Womanhood* argues the only guarantee of woman's happiness is "single blessedness." Flawed and flawless heroines alike must learn to celebrate the cult of domesticity, particularly motherhood.

2.3 Conclusion

In these novels, we begin to see the heroine's coming-of-age arc in publishing. These women characters move from prioritizing caring for the house to their children instead, from equal marriages to chosen single-ness. These "sketches" or "recollections," as suggested by their various titles, seem to imply that a woman's life is made up of moments. Moments of learning to become a flawless woman by supporting their husbands and raising the community's and/or their own children. These sketches contrast the male *bildungsroman*, wherein the hero goes on a quest and grows as an individual.[90] None of these heroines has a career, although the New Woman figure has this opportunity in late nineteenth-century women's fiction. In these early texts, two things remain true: the home should be valued, and marriage, and especially motherhood, are central to American femininity.

It is important to distinguish between the feminine ideology present in early nineteenth-century United States and that of the late nineteenth century. Baym observes that, in the first half of the 1800s, women and men were believed to be capable of the same intellectual accomplishments, if not the same physical ones. Although women's duties remained in the home, "the Enlightenment ideology of republican motherhood" centered on "educated efforts of the head."[91] The Victorian sentimentalism that followed in the second half of the century, assumed that a woman's mind, like her body, was weaker than a man's, placing an emphasis on the spiritual

---

[89] Ibid., p. 210. [90] Sardella-Ayres and Reese, "Where to From Here?," p. 39.
[91] Baym, *American Literary History*, pp. 121–2.

instead, and focusing motherhood on "untutored effusions of the heart."[92] The fictional woman's role shifts from intellectual to emotional and spiritual.

In the above novels, we see the importance of a woman's role in the new country. These protagonists value motherhood, whether or not they are mothers, in part, because, through parenting, they contribute to this new society. This emphasis on motherhood is not lost in girls' literature, but the focus becomes one of a spiritual, not national, imperative. The assumption is that girls will become mothers, because women are best suited for that role. Thus, almost every heroine sacrifices her individual identity in order to fulfill this supposedly higher calling, showing a shift in ideology and publishing.

In spite of some ideological differences, girls' literature has a particular "kinship" with its American predecessors. John Seelye relates orphan girls' literature to its literary "mother," Charlotte Brontë's *Jane Eyre*,[93] and, indeed, there are many comparisons to be drawn between British women's fiction and American girls' novels, as these books were influential on both sides of the Atlantic. However, Avery observes that Sedgwick's heroines share similarities with American girl orphans: both are "[m]eek, much-enduring, yet of far finer material than those about them."[94] Although Avery connects these characteristics to orphan heroines specifically, I would argue that most of the protagonists match this description. Even the flawed heroines are made of "finer material," ready to take on life's challenges with aplomb.

As the nineteenth century continues and the American middle class expands, publishing novels becomes less financially risky. Girls' literature

---

[92] Ibid., p. 122.

[93] J. Seelye, Jane Eyre*'s American Jane Eyre's American Daughters: From The Wide, Wide World to Anne of Green Gables a Study of Marginalized Maidens and What They Mean* (Newark, DE: U of Delaware, 2005).

[94] G. Avery, "Home and family: English and American ideals in the nineteenth century" in D. Butts (ed.), *Stories and Society: Children's Literature in its Social Context* (Houndmills, Basingstoke: Macmillan Academic and Professional, 1992), pp. 37–49, p. 47.

proliferates alongside a general publishing boom, which means an increase in titles as well as an increase in marketing. Publishers put advertisements in magazines, and series books become popular, unlike these women's titles, which often stand alone. As a result, in the following sections, the texts are chosen from a much larger sample.

The emerging girls' literature takes its cue from American women's literature. The same emphasis on motherhood as a woman's opportunity to enact change in the newly formed country, although this time by spiritual means, finds its way into girls' books by 1850. However, the questioning of marriage's suitability and even entertaining the idea of a heroine choosing to "single blessedness" follows later, if at all. The heroines of American nineteenth-century women's novels paved the way for girl heroines of girls' literature: the family story, orphan novel, school story, and African American girls' literature.

3 "Toward that Larger and Less Happy Region of Womanhood": Family Stories

Family stories focus on the domestic lives of girls, often seeing the heroines through to marriage, when they establish homes of their own. In terms of the women's literature in section 2, this genre corresponds most closely to Caroline Gilman's *Recollections of a Southern Matron* (1838); both the mother and father influence Gilman's heroine, creating a legacy for the girls' family stories in this section. Because girls' story protagonists live with their families, they must operate within the family circle and, thus, within the societal bounds of femininity. At the same time, the books often feature so-called flawed heroines who must learn to adapt to these standards, making girlhood a liminal space of freedom in containment. Consequently, these novels simultaneously perform and stretch domestic conventions.

These texts are, in essence, domestic fiction. As Nina Baym notes, the term "domestic" denotes "events taking place in a home setting" and an advocation of "a 'cult of domesticity,' that is, fulfillment for women in marriage and motherhood."[95] This fulfillment is achieved by the fictional woman in Coventry Patmore's poem, *The Angel in the House*,[96] which is emblematic of the second half of the nineteenth century. The angelic figure's patriarchally influenced purpose is to serve the men in her life (her father and later her husband) with "submissiveness, modesty, selflessness," emphasizing a spiritual superiority that stems from "be[ing] angelic."[97] This ideal is present in each of these girls' texts, frequently as a maternal figure and often as the aim of the protagonist's *bildungsroman*. In fact, Ann Douglas refocuses the cult of domesticity as the "cult of motherhood," as society reinforced the belief that a woman's influence must start in

---

[95] Baym, *Woman's Fiction*, p. 26.

[96] C. Patmore, *The Angel in the House* (London: John W. Parker, 1854).

[97] S. Gilbert and S. Gubar, *The Madwoman in the Attic: The Woman Writer and the Nineteenth-Century Literary Imagination*, 2nd ed. (New Haven, CT: Yale University Press, 2000), p. 23.

the home.[98] These heroines are largely headed for the role of wife and mother, and frequently this outcome is achieved in sequels.

Typically, a transformation must first occur, as these heroines are often "tomboys," resembling their fathers more than they do their mothers. The dual emphasis on angelic motherhood as an end goal and the protagonist's relationship to the paternal is central to family stories. As illustrators for children's books "were becoming more prominent toward the end of the [nineteenth] century,"[99] unsurprisingly, these tensions are visually depicted: girls are shown outdoors rather than confined to the domestic indoors, with their fathers or paternal relatives, instead of their mothers, and active, not passive. For example, Figure 2 depicts Jo March ice skating, both outdoors and in motion. This illustrated girlhood differs from the femininity expected of them and perhaps is more exciting than portrayals of girls quietly sewing by a hearth. In spite of these illustrations, the texts emphasize the change to come.

The quintessential family story, or "master text of domestic fiction,"[100] is arguably Alcott's *Little Women* (1868–9), and, in fact, we can see this novel as a blueprint for the family stories that follow. The initial novel was published in 1868, followed by its sequel, *Little Women or Meg, Jo, Beth, and Amy, Part Second* in 1869. As early as 1870, the two parts were published as one volume,[101] encouraging a singular reading of the novels. Many consider Jo to be the protagonist; although one might argue that the four March sisters constitute a collective protagonist.[102] Their distinct personalities contain flaws, such as vanity or tomboy behavior. The text, while focusing on their warm home life, also emphasizes that the girls must overcome these flaws:

[98] A. Douglas, *The Feminization of American Culture* (New York: Alfred A. Knopf, 1977), p. 74.

[99] Tebbel, Vol. II, p. 598.

[100] M. Nikolajeva, *Aesthetic Approaches to Children's Literature* (Latham, MD: Scarecrow Press, 2005), p. 35.

[101] L. Gulliver, *Louisa May Alcott: A Bibliography* (New York: Burt Franklin, 1960), p. 30.

[102] M. Nikolajeva, *From Mythic to Linear: Time in Children's Literature* (Latham, MD: Scarecrow Press, 2000), p. 35.

" Keep near the shore; it isn't safe in the middle." Jo heard, but Amy was just struggling to her feet, and did not catch a word. — PAGE 116.

Figure 2 Louisa May Alcott, *Little Women* (Massachusetts, 1868), np – HathiTrust

their own *Pilgrim's Progress* of sorts, as John Bunyan's 1678 text[103] provides the structure for the 1868 novel. The narrative encourages this perspective, as the novel opens with each heroine receiving a Bible to prepare her for her journey towards feminine perfection. *Little Women* is a blueprint for family fiction published afterwards: there are often several children, mostly girls, in a family. When there are sisters, they follow similar types, such as a vain or angelic sister; however, the text generally focalizes the sister who reforms. Likewise, the importance placed on both Mr. and Mrs. March creates a legacy echoed in later family novels.

Throughout the late nineteenth and into the twentieth centuries, this subgenre of girls' literature was popular, with Alcott's *Little Women* selling its entire first printing of 2,000 copies in only two weeks, and since then, not counting abridged and pirated versions, has sold around 10 million copies.[104] The other novels in this section never reached such popularity or staying power, but they mark the trajectory of the subgenre as the twentieth century dawned. Advertisements use the popularity of *Little Women* to drive sales fifty years after its initial publication. *The Youth's Companion*'s 1918 advertisement of "books that girls like," lists the *Little Women* series first, noting that Alcott's books have "steadily held their own," before detailing recent publications.[105] Various publishers compare their new family story releases to Alcott's novel, in advertisements ranging from 1898[106] to 1921.[107] As the subgenre evolves, the lasting effect of *Little Women* echoes in these novels' plots and in the publishers' advertisements.

This section looks specifically at seven books spanning 1868–1921. Each book has a different publisher, representing the reach of this subgenre in the American book market. While particular publishers do not necessarily come to the forefront, certain authors do. For example, from 1901–19, Carolyn Wells wrote thirty-three children's novels, of which twenty-six

---

[103] J. Bunyan, *Pilgrim's Progress* (London: Nathaniel Ponder, 1678).

[104] A. B. Rioux, *Meg, Jo, Beth, and Amy: The Story of* Little Women *and Why It Still Matters* (New York: W.W. Norton, 2018).

[105] "Advertisement 13," *The Youth's Companion*, 92.42 (1918), p. 544.

[106] "Review 7," *The Bookman; a Review of Books and Life*, 7.3 (1898), p. 255.

[107] "A girl's bookshelf," *New York Times* (13 Nov. 1921), p. BRM9.

were girls' series fiction published by Dodd, Mead, including *Marjorie's Vacation* (1907).[108] Amy Blanchard wrote the series *The Four Corners*[109] and *Dear Little Girl*,[110] both published by G. W. Jacobs, and contributed titles to the *Camp Fire Girls* series (W.A. Wilde).[111] Similarly, Lela Horn Richards wrote the *Caroline* books (Little, Brown), as well as *Henrietta*[112] and *Blue Bonnet* series (Page).[113] These authors each have works examined below. While not a comprehensive look at the many family story novels published during this period, the genre's themes of motherhood and the paternal influence, as first established in *Little Women*, begin to emerge from this sample.

3.1 Mothers

Alcott's *Little Women* contains perhaps the most famous of girls' literature's fictional mothers, Marmee. She guides her daughters to feminine behavior, gently reprimanding Jo about her temper and listening sympathetically to her daughters' troubles. Arguably, the most identifiable illustration from the book is Marmee sitting in a chair, with her daughters gathered around her (Figure 3). That various later editions replicate this image emphasizes Marmee's central nature to the text. She embodies feminine perfection as outlined in the cult of domesticity, reflecting the cultural emphasis on motherhood. As Shirley Foster and Judy Simons observe, the "literature for the young" at this time "promoted the centrality of motherhood in the prevailing social order and the necessity for female self-sacrifice, service, and domestic responsibility."[114] This ideal mother however, often leaves home for a period in the novel, requiring the heroine to step into her place. For example, when Marmee leaves to care for the sick Mr. March, her daughters must run the household, learning self-sacrifice and domestic skills

[108] C. Wells, *Marjorie's Vacation* (New York: Dodd, Mead, 1907).

[109] A. E. Blanchard, *The Four Corners* series (Philadelphia: G.W. Jacobs, 1906–13).

[110] A. E. Blanchard, *Dear Little Girl* series (Philadelphia: G.W. Jacobs, 1897–1924).

[111] A. E. Blanchard, *Camp Fire Girls* series (W.A. Wilde, 1915–17).

[112] L. H. Richards, *Henrietta* series (Boston, MA: Page, 1919–22).

[113] L. H. Richards, *Blue Bonnet* series (Boston, MA: Page, 1914–19).

[114] Foster and Simons, *What Katy Read*, pp. 5–6.

They all drew to the fire, mother in the big chair, with Beth at her feet; Meg and Amy perched on either arm of the chair, and Jo leaning on the back. — PAGE 12.

Figure 3 Louisa May Alcott, *Little Women* (Massachusetts, 1868), frontis-piece – HathiTrust

through necessity. Not all family stories in girls' literature use this feminine ideal as a model. Fictional mothers fall into one of two categories: "Marmees" or the futile "mother."

The ineffective mother is generally introduced with the narrator's description of the eldest daughter (or the protagonist) filling her mother's role by running the household. The family may regard this behavior as normal, but the narrator often critiques her, asserting what is proper. As such, these mother types must reform over the course of the novel; frequently, they are asked to follow their daughters' examples. In this way, both types of mother form their daughters' femininity, either by actively guiding the girls, or by creating a gap in the household for the daughters to fill. Ostensibly motherhood remains centralized in the text. The importance of motherhood marks a difference from the orphan texts examined in section 4, because, either way, the mother is central to the girl's understanding of "proper" femininity, as defined by the cult of domesticity. As Lisa Rowe Fraustino and Karen Coats observe: "[T]he figure of the mother carries an enormous amount of freight across the emotional and intellectual life of a child."[115] This impact remains true for fictional children. Significantly, of the books examined below, Marmee is the only mother to appear with her daughters in the illustrations. This absence highlights the girl's narrative: the mother figure represents the restricted adult femininity that awaits, not the adventures of girlhood.

Thirty-eight years after *Little Women*, Amy E. Blanchard's *The Four Corners* (1906)[116] features a mother in the tradition of Marmee. The cover of *Four Corners* (Figure 4) illustrates the mother's absence, depicting only the four daughters: the oldest at the top, with her three sisters beneath her. Mrs. Corner is portrayed as an industrious mother who guides her four daughters with love. Mr. Corner died before the novel, and so it is up to

---

[115] L. R. Fraustino and K. Coats, "Mothers Wanted" in L. R. Fraustino and K. Coats (eds.), *Mothers in Children's and Young Adult Literature: From Eighteenth Century to Postfeminism* (Jackson, MS: University of Mississippi Press, 2016), pp. 3–24, p. 3.

[116] A. E. Blanchard, *The Four Corners* (Philadelphia: G.W. Jacobs, 1906).

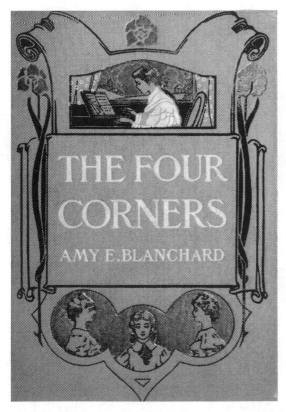

Figure 4 Amy Blanchard, *Four Corners* (Pennsylvania, 1906), cover –
HathiTrust

Mrs. Corner, along with her aunt Sarah, to provide for the household.
Although they live in a sort of genteel poverty (they still have two
servants), they appear to be a happy family. However, to help center Nan
as the focus of the book series, Mrs. Corner leaves for the Adirondacks for
her health and asks Nan to fill her place. Mrs. Corner tells her: "[Y]ou are
my eldest and my staff to lean upon, you must try to help me bear [these

responsibilities] without rebelling."[117] Nan does so with success, for although the text critiques her sentimental nature, she also likes "nothing better than to whirl in and help in domestic emergencies."[118] What chapter 4 heralds as "A Mother's Secret," quickly gives way to chapter 5: "Housewifely Cares." Chapter 4's last line alludes to this transition, noting that Nan "felt that her young spirit was stretching beyond the limits of childhood toward that larger and less happy region of womanhood."[119] Nan's responsibilities diminish when her aunt returns home; however, Nan assumes motherly authority when discussing her sister's behavior with their teacher or planning Christmas festivities. She dons the mantle of motherhood, preparing herself for womanhood, only because of Mrs. Corner's absence.

Another angelic, yet removed mother occurs in Wells' *Marjorie's Vacation*. Heroine Marjorie spends the summer at her maternal grandmother's farm. Similar to *The Four Corners*, a female relative serves as a temporary mother figure, or what might be termed othermothering.[120] Akin to the republican marriage, Julie Pfeiffer defines othermothering as the "need to share the nurturing and mentoring of children," which "decenters heterosexual models of power in favor of community mothering and mentoring."[121] Marjorie's othermother furthers the idea that "girls need more and different mothering than they receive from their biological mothers."[122] As Pfeiffer sees it, the othermother helps usher the adolescent girl into maturity, where marriage will mark her success. For Marjorie, her grandmother guides her, teaching her proper femininity. Marjorie's

---

[117] Ibid., p. 68. [118] Ibid., p. 14. [119] Ibid., p. 83.

[120] This theory stems from African American communities, wherein often women care for one another's children and are thus symbols of power. See R. R. Troester, "Turbulence and tenderness: Mothers, daughters, and 'othermothers' in Paule Marshall's *Brown Girl, Brownstones*," *SAGE: A Scholarly Journal on Black Women*, 1.2 (1984), 13–16.

[121] J. Pfeiffer, "The Romance of Othermothering in *Backfisch* Books" in L. R. Fraustino and K. Coats (eds.), *Mothers in Children's and Young Adult Literature: From Eighteenth Century to Postfeminism* (Jackson, MS: University of Mississippi Press, 2016), pp. 59–74, p. 61.

[122] Ibid., p. 61.

character echoes that of Jo March, as she spends the majority of the novel causing trouble and reaping the consequences. Marjorie's curls refuse to lie flat and ladylike, a metaphor for Marjorie's own difficulties in adhering to feminine standards. Four of the five text illustrations feature Marjorie in action, such as climbing up a ladder into her treehouse and climbing to the top of the cupboard (Figure 5).

Throughout the novel, she and her grandmother talk about the importance of Marjorie obeying, but Marjorie's consistent defense is that her grandmother never directly forbade Marjorie do that action. The narrator observes: "[I]t seemed to be natural for her to get into mischief,"[123] implying that the feminine behavior Marjorie's grandmother wants for Marjorie is *unnatural* for her. Yet the novel's end implies that Marjorie eventually will acquire feminine ways. When Marjorie's friends realize that they will be sixteen on Marjorie's return, she responds that, as young ladies, "we won't get into such mischief."[124] The word "mischief" has childish connotations, defined by the Oxford English Dictionary as "a person (esp. a child) who causes petty annoyance or acts in a naughty or vexatious manner."[125] This emphasis on childhood is echoed in Marjorie's acknowledgement that she will assume the role her othermother desires for her.

These idealized, absent mothers are the opposite of the physically present, but ineffectual mother figures of other family stories. In these novels, the mother figure is often accustomed to a privileged lifestyle, leaving the father (and as a result the children) to work to ensure her life remains "easy." Generally, over the course of the novel, the mother must change, but often not before her daughters have assumed the angelic role already. This trope speaks to a broader context of motherhood in the nineteenth century: "fears about motherhood gone awry," which texts answered by "imagining ways for girls to take care of other girls, the men and boys around them, and even mothers themselves."[126] In these stories,

---

[123] Ibid., p. 115. [124] Ibid., p. 290.

[125] "[M]ischief, n." *Oxford English Dictionary Online*, Oxford University Press, March 2020, www.oed.com/view/Entry/119293.

[126] Sanders, *Disciplining Girls*, p. 162.

"Though it required some scrambling, she
finally reached the top"

Figure 5 Carolyn Wells, *Marjorie's Vacation* (New York, 1907), np –
HathiTrust

by proving their mothering capability, the heroines prove their inclination
towards a more idealized womanhood than their mothers inhabited.

In Gene Stratton Porter's *A Girl of the Limberlost* (1909),[127] the protagonist Elnora Comstock lives with her emotionally distant mother. Her
mother's behavior is blamed on Mr. Comstock's drowning in the swamp
during Elnora's birth, which prevented Mrs. Comstock from saving him.

---

[127] G. Stratton Porter, *A Girl of the Limberlost* (New York: Doubleday, Page, 1909).

While Elnora's neighbors, including an othermother, frequently try to help her, Mrs. Comstock often dissuades them, leaving Elnora to provide for herself. When Elnora enters society, by attending the local high school and befriending her peers, her mother occasionally bakes treats for Elnora to share. Elnora and her neighbors make excuses for Mrs. Comstock, blaming her behavior on grief. It is not until Mrs. Comstock ruins Elnora's chance at college that she takes an interest in Elnora's lucrative moth-hunting hobby, and, as a result, an interest in Elnora herself. Mrs. Comstock's contact with nature is the catalyst in her transformation and, as such, is illustrated (the only other visually depicted mother in these seven novels): the picture shows Mrs. Comstock looking at a moth, speaking to her dead husband wistfully about how he might have lived differently following a similar revelation (Figure 6). Although not depicted, Elnora serves as the bridge between her mother and the natural world. This image has a different message than that of Marmee surrounded by her daughters. Marmee does not need a moth-inspired epiphany, as she already is the heart of her family and illustrated as such.

The final step in Mrs. Comstock's change comes when Elnora must teach instead of attend college. Her mother rents a house in town (establishing their place in society) and troublingly, bleaches her sun-weathered skin to better adhere to "delicate porcelain white"[128] femininity. With her mother's transformation, Elnora is ushered into the cult of domesticity. Even her chosen husband encourages a diminutive form of femininity, insisting that her personality would be ruined by a college education, thereby cementing Elnora's place in the home.

In Nell Speed's *The Carter Girls* (1917),[129] Mrs. Carter also fails to meet the angel-in-the-house model. Instead of being an active mother or help-mate to her husband, she is purely ornamental. She is described as a "beauty" with "daintiness and charm,"[130] emphasizing her high social standing. While away, she writes her daughters about their clothing and the proper way to treat the servants, rather than the more pressing matters, such as budgeting, about which the girls are worried. Her inability to act as an

---

[128] Ibid., p. 352. [129] N. Speed, *The Carter Girls* (New York: A.L. Burt, 1917).
[130] Ibid., p. 12.

"' If you had known about wonders like these in the
days of your youth, Robert Comstock, could you
ever have done the thing you did ?' "

Figure 6 Gene Stratton Porter, *A Girl of the Limberlost* (New York, 1909),
np – HathiTrust

effective wife and mother is encapsulated by the observation: Mrs. Carter is "more like the elder sister of her great girls than like their mother."[131] The text critiques this resemblance, repeatedly stating that in order for her husband to recover fully, Mrs. Carter must change. She eventually confesses to her children "what a poor wife I have been to him and foolish mother to all of you."[132] Even her letter of repentance demonstrates Mrs. Carter's failure to comprehend their financial situation, recommending her daughters buy clothes to outfit their business venture. She may have recognized the error of her ways, but unlike her daughters, who limit their spending and earn additional income during their parents' absence, Mrs. Carter is unable to become the financial partner her husband needs, echoing the mother in Sedgwick's *A New-England Tale*. As Baym observes, "encomiums on the female New England character focus on rationality, self-control, industry, frugality."[133] It is Mrs. Carter's daughters, not Mrs. Carter, who demonstrate these practical traits, preparing them for marriage.

The latest book examined in this section, Lela Horn Richards' *Then Came Caroline* (1921),[134] is perhaps the most prominent example of this occurrence. Readers follow the *bildungsroman* of Caroline, the second youngest daughter in the prominent Ravenel family. Drawing many parallels to *Little Women*, there are five sisters, each of whom has a distinct personality. For example, the eldest sister Leigh has a curved spine, but despite her weakened condition, Leigh assists their doctor father, runs the household, and serves as the othermother for her younger sisters. Disability or disease is often characterized as an especially feminine characteristic. Lois Keith observes that this femininity is, in part, due to physical restrictions, that this "saintly" woman "was always where she should be; in the home, providing comfort and solace to others. But she could never seek to fulfill her own dreams and ambitions."[135] Leigh's sacrificial behavior eventually leads to a breakdown. At which point, Caroline intervenes, pressing her

---

[131] Ibid. [132] Ibid., p. 146. [133] Baym, *American Literary History*, p. 170.

[134] L. H. Richards, *Then Came Caroline* (Boston, MA: Little, Brown, 1921).

[135] L. Keith, *Take Up Thy Bed and Walk: Death, Disability and Cure in Classic Fiction for Girls* (London: Women's Press, 2001), p. 82.

mother to resume the role that she had long since abdicated to Leigh. In the process, Caroline assumes some of the feminine burden, becoming "the head of the house"[136] and ushering the previously boisterous Caroline into the cult of domesticity.

With each of these novels, the mother is instrumental in the heroine's journey into a demure femininity. So-called bad mothers are as important as good mothers in girls' family stories, allowing othermothers to guide the heroine. In this way, these stories claim that a girl needs an ideal mother figure to guide her into womanhood. Interestingly, these books divide chronologically, with earlier family stories containing idealized mothers and later ones featuring the ineffective ones. This departure could be a result of the relatively small amount of texts analyzed, but there is also a chance this trend serves as a warning for readers as the freer New Woman figure emerges in women's fiction, encouraging girl readers to follow the path of the heroine, rather than risk becoming bad mothers themselves. In addition to mothers, fathers are also central to the heroine's *bildungsroman*.

3.2 Fathers

As was the case with early American women's literature, motherhood, in both its presence and absence, is central to these family stories. However, many of the protagonists in these family stories have noted resemblances to their fathers, or their father's family, and these paternal connections often are the root of their flaws and/or make them outsiders in their immediate families. In this sense, we can see the paternal emphasis as somewhat subversive, pushing against what Douglas calls the cult of motherhood. When a father is featured in the illustrations, it is generally in a moment of affection towards the protagonist, such as Beth running towards newly-arrived-home Mr. March (Figure 7). These depictions mark an interesting shift in perceived girls' literature, as Foster and Simons in their examination of canonical girls' literature note "the gradual disappearance of fathers or father-figures form the novels" as actual nineteenth-century fathers increasingly worked outside the home.[137] More specifically, Avery observes that

---

[136] Richards, *Then Came Caroline*, p. 252.
[137] Foster and Simons, *What Katy Read*, p. 7.

But it was too late; the study-door flew open, and Beth ran straight into her father's arms. — PAGE 320.

Figure 7 Louisa May Alcott, *Little Women* (Massachusetts, 1868), np – HathiTrust

"contempt for the father is curiously prevalent in the American family story."[138] Although occasionally fathers are "loved and respected," they remain "secondary" to the more central mothers.[139] While my own findings do not corroborate Avery's claims, he is occasionally absent, which might account for his supposed secondary role. However, whether present or absent, the father is frequently regarded as a beloved, if not favored, figure in the heroine's life, thus holding a prominent place in his daughter's life.

With Mr. March as a background figure, his absence serves as a presence and narrative catalyst for the majority of *Little Women, Part First*. Jo refers to herself as "the man of the family now Papa is away."[140] Jo readily assumes this role as it better suits her "tomboy" preferences. She frequently bemoans her gender, which prevents her from fighting in the war or attending college. Even Jo's feminine sacrifice leads to a masculine association: in order to send money to Mr. March, Jo sells her long hair, leaving "a curly crop" that is "boyish" and "becoming."[141] For Jo "boyish" and "becoming" are not contradictions. However, by the end of *Part First*, Mr. March returns and pronounces Jo changed. He marks Jo's entrance into the patriarchally approved femininity: "I rather miss my wild girl, but if I get a strong, helpful, tenderhearted woman in her place, I shall feel quite satisfied."[142] Unlike the other family stories in this chapter, in part Jo's father's absence ushers Jo into a feminine womanhood, ready for the marriage awaiting her in *Part Second*.

In Richards' *Then Came Caroline*, Caroline shares distinct similarities to Jo March, in that she begins the story a somewhat "wild" ten-year-old. However, through trials – such as her younger sister's death and their genteel poverty – Caroline steps into the role of feminine duty. Similar to the early women's novels, there is a clear patriotic strain throughout the novel; for example, Caroline has playmates in the middle and lower classes. She continually identifies with her father, who encourages these "democratic" inclinations.[143] Their relationship is central to the text, as demonstrated by the frontispiece illustration (Figure 8), featuring Caroline sitting

---

[138] Avery, *Behold the Child*, p. 164. [139] Ibid., p. 165.
[140] Alcott, *Little Women*, p. 14. [141] Ibid., p. 132. [142] Ibid., p. 176.
[143] Richards, *Then Came Caroline*, pp. 185, 250.

"But most of all I want to live—to understand
people." FRONTISPIECE. *See page 301.*

Figure 8 Lela Horn Richards, *Then Came Caroline* (Massachusetts, 1921),
frontispiece – HathiTrust

at her father's feet. Her father, rather than her mother, oversees Caroline's
discipline and personal development, further aligning Caroline with the
paternal. The text repeatedly refers to her nonresemblance to her Southern

aristocratic mother's family, and instead favoring her father's family, also Southern, who lack wealth and prestige. Regardless, the Ravenel surname is prominently connected to the southern United States, dating back to the seventeenth century.[144] Whether Caroline is related to this particular family is unknown, but readers might recognize the name's American heritage. At the end of the novel, Caroline's maternal great-aunt invites her to move to England. Caroline refuses her great-aunt's charity, wanting to remain dependent only on her father: "I have a nasty pride, I reckon; it's the Ravenel in me, I suspect."[145] She instead stays in the United States, under her father's guidance, cementing her connection to her father and his family.

For Stratton Porter's *A Girl of the Limberlost*, Elnora Comstock's relationship to her deceased father is more tenuous. For the most part, their connection exists through the violin. Unaware that her father played the instrument, Elnora discovers her natural talent. Only when she establishes that connection, does she learn details about her father, how he too "played [the violin] like a master."[146] Her othermother gives Elnora two gifts: knowledge of her father and his violin. When Mrs. Comstock first hears Elnora play the violin, she believes "[t]he swamp had sent back the soul of her loved dead and put in into the body of the daughter she resented."[147] This revelation is the catalyst that leads to Mrs. Comstock finally loving Elnora: she "banishe[s]" "every tangible evidence of [Elnora's] father" so that Elnora is "at last ... allowed to take his place."[148] After this action, Mr. Comstock's good qualities live on in Elnora, and the mother–daughter relationship is restored.

The father is also the driving force of the plot in Speed's *Carter Girls*. His illness is the reason the oldest, Douglas becomes "the head and guiding star of the family," with "[h]er father's burden ... falling on her young shoulders."[149] Masculine duties are emphasized here; however, because Douglas is conveniently not "of age," Dr. Wright, their legal guardian, becomes a pseudo-father figure. This interloper is viewed unfavorably by

[144] H. E. Ravenel, *Ravenel Records*, (Atlanta, GA: Franklin Printing and Publishing., 1898), p. 35.
[145] Richards, *Then Came Caroline*, p. 305. [146] Stratton Porter, *Limberlost*, p. 177.
[147] Ibid., p. 208. [148] Ibid., p. 261. [149] Speed, *Carter Girls*, p. 153.

Helen, the arguable protagonist, who considers herself her father's favorite. Helen aligns herself with her father and the masculine, challenging Dr. Wright's guidance. Her so-called tomboy qualities, such as being headstrong and outspoken, underscore Helen's behavior throughout the novel, especially in relation to Dr. Wright. Notably, Helen is not allowed to remain in this masculine state. Their mother's absence forces Helen to fill a maternal role, by quitting school to focus on domestic tasks. Then an injury puts her in a vulnerable position, her dependence feminizing her, as Dr. Wright simultaneously saves Helen and becomes her love interest. In spite of Helen's activeness throughout the book – she and her sisters run a camp – the frontispiece (Figure 9) shows Dr. Wright carrying her. Thus, Helen's connection to her father is erased, and in a moment of oedipal completion, she falls in love with her pseudo-father.

In Blanchard's *The Four Corners*, Nan's connection to her father's family comes first from her name, which she shares with a paternal aunt. Her paternal grandmother observes that Nan has her father's eyes and smile, as well as the "Corner fingers,"[150] furthering this link. She also shares her paternal aunt Helen's dreamy countenance, about which her maternal aunt Sarah complains. Nan actively engages with her sisters and peers in most of the illustrations, except for one: she is outside playing her pretend piano (a skill her aunt Helen shares), meeting that same aunt for the first time. As the first illustration (Figure 10), it highlights the importance of Nan's connection to her paternal relatives. Because of a long-past argument, Nan's immediate family are not in contact with the Corners or their fortune. Nan initiates the reconciliation. Naturally, her younger sister Jack, named for their father, is the next to extend an olive branch. Despite Nan's mother's approval (albeit from afar), her own namesake, Mary Lee, is the last of the children to reconcile, further emphasizing the divide between the paternal and maternal sides. Nan succeeds in reuniting them, so that Aunt Helen moves in with them, bringing the Corner family money. Using her paternal resemblance, Nan has successfully bridged the familial strife, leading to a better life for her immediate family.

---

[150] Blanchard, *Four Corners*, p. 204.

"Would it hurt me to walk? I can't bear to be so much
trouble"—*Page* 258

Figure 9 Nell Speed, *The Carter Girls* (New York, 1917), frontispiece –
Library of Congress

A unique outlier to family stories' parental relationships occurs in
Annie Fellows Johnston's *Little Colonel* series (1895–1912). Although
the heroine Lloyd Sherman has both parents, the central relationship,

SHE SEATED HERSELF BEFORE HER LOG PIANO AND BEGAN
HER SONG

Figure 10 Amy Blanchard, *Four Corners* (Pennsylvania, 1906), np – HathiTrust

particularly in the first novel,[151] is between Lloyd and her maternal grandfather, known as the Colonel. In fact, her nickname (and the series title) comes from her resemblance to him. Lloyd, who bears her grandfather's surname as her first name, is frequently described as having his

[151] A. F. Johnston, *The Little Colonel* (Boston, MA: L.C. Page, 1895).

"vile temper."[152] This emotion is the antithesis of idealized femininity and thus, marriageability. Pratt argues: "The supreme goal of these novels of development is to groom the young hero for marriage," thus, "young girls are given tests in submission."[153] In this light, the unsubmissive Lloyd remarkably differs from other heroines. As Sardella-Ayres posits, "Lloyd's temper is not presented as a fault to overcome" but "earns her a welcome into the Lloyd family home."[154] Lloyd embraces her gender incongruity, declaring, "I de'pise to be a little lady."[155] The majority of the illustrations reflect her masculine affinity, depicting Lloyd interacting with her grandfather: defying him, standing affectionately beside him, and wearing his colonel's hat.

In spite of this pervasive connection between Lloyd and the Colonel, the text emphasizes the feminine, hinting towards Lloyd's future womanhood: Lloyd returns to her mother's childhood home, lives in her maternal grandmother's cottage, and plays with her mother's childhood doll. The emphasis is on the maternal and the "angelic," a word used to describe both her mother and grandmother. The last illustration notably shows Lloyd mirroring her grandmother's portrait, on which her gaze rests (Figure 11). Much like Jo March's eventual change, this final illustration points towards Lloyd's future change into a "passive, symbolic creature."[156] Lloyd's transformation occurs gradually over the ten-book series, with some of the biggest changes happening in *The Little Colonel at Boarding-School* (1903),[157] where school socializes her into proper femininity. In *The Little Colonel's Knight Comes Riding* (1907), her transformation culminates: wearing her grandmother's wedding gown, Lloyd "put[s] on the sweet shy

---

[152] Ibid., p. 11.   [153] Pratt, *Archetypal Patterns*, p. 14.

[154] D. Sardella-Ayres, "Rewriting and re-whiting *The Little Colonel*: Racial anxieties, tomboyism, and Lloyd Sherman," *Children's Literature*, 47 (2019), 79–103, pp. 85, 88.

[155] Johnston, *Little Colonel*, p. 28.

[156] Sardella-Ayres, "Rewriting and re-whiting *The Little Colonel*," p. 102, n. 13.

[157] A. F. Johnston, *The Little Colonel at Boarding-School* (Boston, MA, L.C. Page, 1903).

Figure 11 Annie Fellows Johnston, *Little Colonel* (Massachusetts, 1895), p.187 – Library of Congress

manner that had been the charm of its first wearer."[158] Lloyd now resembles

[158] A. F. Johnston, *The Little Colonel's Knight Comes Riding* (Boston, MA: L.C. Page, 1907), p. 142.

her idealized, hyper-feminine grandmother, instead of her hyper-masculine grandfather, and, ultimately, remains connected to the maternal side of the family.

As with Lloyd Sherman, most of these texts feature girls who, in spite of their masculine or paternal connections, grow to be ideal women and mothers. They follow in the footsteps of the quintessential family story heroine, Jo March, who, as Elaine Showalter observes, "has given up, or at least postponed, her dream of becoming a great author in exchange for marriage and motherhood."[159] Jo is made over to fit the angel-in-the-house model, and so too must each family-story heroine step into the role outlined by the cult of domesticity. Her tomboyish ways end with girlhood, a freedom bound to that liminal period, that while perhaps adding pleasure to the girl's life at that time, inevitably must be sacrificed: "the American female['s] carefree girlhood ended abruptly in staid and drab matronhood."[160] The illustrations of activity and the outdoors give way to illustrations of wedding dresses and home.

In some ways, these tomboy qualities are central to the American myth. Their traits, what might be described as "pluck," exist in girlhood in order to buoy a particular American womanhood. In her work exploring fictional American tomboys, Michelle Ann Abate traces "strong, gender-defiant women have been a longstanding hallmark of the United States" from the pilgrims to the pioneers.[161] These tomboy heroines may grow up to be "staid and drab" matrons, but they have a legacy of pluck. Indeed, we see evidence of this resilience in illustrations. In *Little Women, Part Second*, Jo is only depicted in nature or writing inside; even in her domestication, Jo pushes back (in illustrations at least) against restrictive femininity. Perhaps these paratexts provide what is impossible to write or publish, an alternative femininity for the protagonist. Authors were limited by what publishers thought would sell. Readers wanted Jo to marry, in spite of Alcott's desire for Jo to remain a "literary spinster"; therefore, Alcott's publisher requested

---

[159] E. Showalter, *A Jury of Her Peers: American Woman Writers from Anne Bradstreet to Annie Proulx* (New York: Alfred A. Knopf, 2009), p. 143.

[160] Welter, *Dimity Convictions*, p. 9. [161] Abate, *Tomboys*, p. xiv.

this ending.[162] The written narratives, however, continue to encourage just one view of femininity, ultimately encouraged by fictional fathers and mothers. However, familial guidance is not the only way texts encourage girls to adhere to societal feminine standards. Orphan heroines must enter the cult of domesticity without a mother's example.

---

[162] Foster and Simons, *What Katy Read*, p. 92.

4 "The Joys of Being an Orphan": Orphan Girls' Stories

Outside children's literature staples, like Alcott's *Little Women* (1868–9), orphan stories remain one of the most popular subgenres of girls' narratives. Some of these novels are still in print, such as Kate Douglas Wiggin's *Rebecca of Sunnybrook Farm* (1903) and Eleanor Porter's *Pollyanna* (1913), each of which has sold over 1 million copies in the United States.[163] As children's books, orphan texts have unprecedented popularity. Their appeal, perhaps, is their sentiment, echoing Sedgwick's orphan novel, *A New-England Tale*, but, arguably, readers also are drawn to the freedom bestowed on the heroines, which is beyond what many readers could obtain.

Claudia Mills posits the way in which an orphan's experience and desires are in juxtaposition: "The orphan child represents pure possibility, freedom from family ties that chafe and bind. Yet almost every orphan novel in the end is about the search for a family."[164] To be a girl is still limited by societal expectations, but girls without a family do not abide by quite the same rules. However, because, as Mills notes, the heroine seeks (and eventually finds) a family, the novel's *bildungsroman* becomes one of fitting into the societal role offered to girls and women, namely, the cult of domesticity. For this reason, her agency, while greater than those in the family stories, is still limited, as her trajectory ends in the domestic. Thus, the goal of this subgenre is – to borrow from Judith Rowbotham – to teach mostly good little girls to become good little wives.[165] Similar to what Annis Pratt observes about the "woman's *bildungsroman*," in orphan girls' novels, "we find a genre that pursues the opposite of its generic intent – it provides models for 'growing down' rather than for 'growing up.'"[166]

---

[163] Tebbel, Vol. II, pp. 652, 653.

[164] C. Mills, "Children in search of a family: Orphan novels through the century," *Children's Literature in Education*, 18.4 (1987), 227–39, p. 227.

[165] J. Rowbotham, *Good Girls Make Good Wives: Guidance for Girls in Victorian Fiction* (Oxford: Blackwell Publishing, 1989).

[166] Pratt, *Archetypal Patterns*, p. 14.

This growth pattern often means that the heroine loses agency and freedom in the process of becoming a woman. Her individual identity is replaced by a communal one, as the heroine's focus shifts from personal aspirations to domestic fulfillment. In illustrations, we generally see the heroine moving from the outdoors to inside, a visual representation of this transformation. She enters the cult of domesticity, where her voice softens or silences and her identity centers around motherhood and wifehood. As a result, this subgenre works to prepare readers for a similar trajectory, an eventual sacrifice of their individuality for the feminine roles dictated by society.

Each of the orphan girls' novels included in this section centers around a female protagonist who is missing one or both parents. Most of the heroines have no mother, or their mothers have relinquished custody. Because of motherhood's importance in nineteenth-century literature, I argue that not having a present mother, or having a permanently removed mother, qualifies as orphanhood. As Abate notes, most fictional tomboys from this era either have no mother or their mother is "emotionally absent."[167] Tomboys arguably have more agency, as they do not conform to society's prescription for passive femininity: "Without mothers to indoctrinate them in women's traditional gender roles, they are able to define these elements for themselves."[168] Abate's theorized trajectory for the nineteenth-century tomboy aligns with my analysis of the orphan girl. Of course, Abate specifically focuses on the tomboy figure, and not all orphaned heroines are tomboys. The similarity is that many orphans, lacking a mother, initially do not assume socially approved feminine behaviors. Thus, the *bildungsroman* for tomboys and orphans includes them learning and eventually adhering to nineteenth-century feminine standards.

The orphan girls' novels examined here were published between 1850 and 1936. Because this subgenre contains the most "classic" novels, the texts examined here are generally well known, both in criticism and on bookstore shelves. As with family stories, the publishers of orphan girls' novels are

---

[167] Abate, *Tomboys*, p. xviii. [168] Ibid., p. xix.

varied. No publisher is repeated, sequels withstanding. Publishing connections emerge: for example, the 1872 *What Katy Did* shares publisher Robert Brothers with the seminal *Little Women* (1868–9). *Elsie Dinsmore*'s publisher, M.W. Dodd eventually became Dodd, Mead, which published Carolyn Wells' family stories. *Pollyanna*'s publisher, L.C. Page, also published girls' literature by Canadian author L. M. Montgomery. As with family stories, authors, not publishers, appear to be the commonality between orphan girls' texts, particularly as many are series; *Elsie Dinsmore* is the first of twenty-eight books and *What Katy Did*, the first of five. *Rebecca of Sunnybrook Farm* (Houghton, Mifflin), *Pollyanna*, and *Roller Skates* (Viking Press) are the first of two books, and their respective authors wrote a range of other girls' texts unrelated to those series.

The first half of this section examines heroines who use their agency to change others, while the second half features heroines who themselves must change. These orphans begin their novels with varying degrees of agency, but they share what Pratt calls their growing down.

4.1 Orphans who Influence Change

Several orphan girls' stories feature heroines who mold the adults (usually mother figures) into better mothers. Although the heroines might change over the course of the novel or series, the parents' transformation is more dramatic. These fictional girls arguably have a consider amount of agency, entering their new homes with their own ideas. They act on their own terms, but their sway lies in their ideal behavior and/or loving the parent figure unconditionally, both somewhat passive actions, aligning with the influence touted by the cult of domesticity.

Martha Finley's *Elsie Dinsmore* series (1867–1905) is one of the longest running girls' series written by a single author. Over the course of the first two novels, *Elsie Dinsmore* (1867) and *Elsie's Holidays at Roselands* (1868),[169]

---

[169] The two novels were written as one volume, but the publisher divided them.

Elsie is reunited with her father, Mr. Dinsmore, who is often overbearing towards his young daughter. Elsie's strong Christian faith guides her actions. However, in spite of the text's emphasis on humility and deference to authority, Elsie uses her faith to disobey those, often her father, who ask her to behave in contrast to her interpretation of the Bible. This theme is so pervasive that the only illustration in the book (Figure 12) features such an instance: Elsie passed out on the floor after refusing to play a nonreligious song on a Sunday. While this image shows Elsie immobile, and, therefore, seeming to lack agency, in those moments of physical weakness Elsie is the most influential. For example, in *Roselands*, Elsie refuses when Mr. Dinsmore asks her to read from a nonreligious book on a Sunday. In spite of the rift (and multiple consequences) that occur, Elsie never repents, and, in the end, she triumphs. Elsie's illness becomes so dire that the doctor declares her dead, leaving Mr. Dinsmore to repent. Soon thereafter, the doctor realizes that Elsie is, in fact, alive, but Mr. Dinsmore remains a convert to Elsie's Christianity. These two events encapsulate Elsie's role in the series. She may be young and female, but she is authoritative, in part due to wealth and religion. In orphan girls' literature, Elsie is the exception in that her femininity wholly aligns with the cult of domesticity.

While today the series is less well known outside conservative Christian groups,[170] it was quite popular at the time of its publication. In fact, "for more than three generations [Finley's] *Elsie Dinsmore* outsold every other juvenile book with the exception of *Little Women*."[171] The *Elsie* series is mentioned frequently, often with disdain, in twentieth-century girls' novels (*When Patty Went to College*, 1903; *Roller Skates*, 1936; *Betsy in Spite of Herself*, 1946). Although the heavy-handed religious fervor is ridiculed, such references highlight Elsie's popularity.

---

[170] Recent editions are released by Christian publishers, such as Hendrickson Publishers.

[171] M. S. Smedman, "Martha Finley (26 April 1828–30 January 1909)" in G. E. Estes (ed.), *American Writers for Children Before 1900* (Detroit: Gale Research, 1985), pp. 177–85, p. 179.

Figure 12 Martha Finley, *Elsie Dinsmore* (New York, 1867), frontispiece – HathiTrust

As the nineteenth century progresses, Christianity becomes less of a focus in girls' literature, and, as a result, the heroines themselves begin to look different. The influence they have over their new homes becomes more secular, one of general "childhood joy" or optimism, rather than religious tenets. Of these heroines is Wiggin's eponymous *Rebecca of Sunnybrook Farm*. Rebecca Randall, although she has a mother, is sent to live with her two aunts to help alleviate the family's finances. Unlike Elsie's religious fervor, Rebecca's passion is for life. Her talkativeness and boisterousness positively influences her aunts' lives. Her aunt Miranda, in turn, tries to "put her on the right track" towards what we might assume is "proper" femininity, or "the making of Rebecca."[172] By the novel's end, Rebecca assumes the feminine role of caretaker by nursing her sick mother. She is rewarded, inheriting her aunts' home on Miranda's death. The text implies that Rebecca will take Miranda's place: she will be the heart of the home, adhering to Miranda's training while maintaining her joyous nature. Bookending the novel are her drives to the house, which demonstrate her development: on her first drive, Rebecca talks incessantly, but her last is characterized by "silence."[173] Her silence is in part grief-driven but also a mark of adulthood. There are no illustrations in this book, but the cover image shows a house, the domestic place Rebecca inherits. Rebecca's agency is diminished as she welcomes her family into the home to care for them, growing down in the process.

In a similar vein, Porter's *Pollyanna* tells the story of the eponymous heroine who teaches the town of Beldingsville the glad game. Porter's novel ran through fifteen printings in its first year. Much like Rebecca, Pollyanna is a romantic child, bringing gladness to those around her. In *Pollyanna*, change happens only to those around her. Likewise, the illustrations depict many of the interactions between Pollyanna and those whom she transforms, including Aunt Polly, Mr. Pendleton, Jimmy Bean, and Mrs. Snow. Much like Aunt Miranda, so Aunt Polly, Pollyanna's cold, maiden aunt, comes to love Pollyanna, but only after an automobile crash leaves Pollyanna paralyzed. Aunt Polly, not Pollyanna, joins the cult of domesticity, becoming the mother figure that Pollyanna needs, as well as a wife through reconciling with her former beau.

However, there remains a sense that Pollyanna must eventually cast off her childish way of telling adults of her glad game. In Porter's sequel,

---

[172] K. D. Wiggin, *Rebecca of Sunnybrook Farm* (Boston, MA: Houghton, Mifflin, 1903), pp. 31, 6.

[173] Ibid., p. 324.

Pollyanna Grows Up (1915),[174] Pollyanna enters adulthood. The novel
features a conversation that perhaps supersedes the audience's feelings
about Pollyanna as an adult, that "somehow, I don't think – I ever wanted
Pollyanna to grow up."[175] In anticipation of seeing her, her childhood
friend Jimmy Bean and Mr. Pendleton express concern that she will have
changed too drastically, while acknowledging that "I couldn't fancy
a grown-up Pollyanna perpetually admonishing people to be glad for
something."[176] Pollyanna manages to walk this line with some success in
the novel. She is quieter now, and she only mentions the glad game when
admonishing herself. Her change directives are now inward, to better fulfill
the cult of domesticity. She hosts friends in a hotel she sets up in her home,
cooking, cleaning, and caring for them as guests. By the end of the novel,
she has proved herself ready to marry Jimmy Bean and officially enter
womanhood. The illustrations show her readiness, as each time she is
depicted with Jimmy they are inside, in a domestic space (Figure 13), in
contrast to the illustrations with the other man, Jamie, which are set
outdoors (Figure 14). Despite her romantic, even idealized childhood in
the first novel, in the tradition of orphan girls' novels, Pollyanna changes in
order to better adhere to social standards of the day. She must "grow
down." Pollyanna and Rebecca mark the transition from orphans who
enact change in others and those who themselves change, as in many
ways they do both.

4.2 Orphans who Change

Part of being an orphan is having a level of freedom, particularly when it
comes to societal expectations, but before entering womanhood, the orphan
must learn to comply with these standards. Arguably, the first girls' book
published was Warner's *The Wide, Wide World*. Warner was a popular
author, averaging about 150,000 annual book sales.[177] Her first novel, *The
Wide, Wide World*, led the way, as it "immediately began selling in figures
which astonished everyone": "thirteen editions in two years" and eventually "more than 500,000 copies [sold] in America alone."[178] Like early

---

[174] E. H. Porter, *Pollyanna Grows Up* (Boston, MA: L.C. Page, 1915).
[175] Ibid., p. 153. [176] Ibid., p. 154. [177] Tebbel, Vol. I, p. 543. [178] Ibid., p. 308.

"JIMMY LOOKED DOWN AT THE WISTFUL, EAGER FACE."
(*See page 184.*)

Figure 13 Eleanor Porter, *Pollyanna Grows Up* (Massachusetts, 1915), frontispiece – HathiTrust

" ' THE INSTRUMENT THAT YOU PLAY ON, POLLYANNA,
WILL BE THE GREAT HEART OF THE WORLD.' "

Figure 14 Eleanor Porter, *Pollyanna Grows Up* (Massachusetts, 1915), np –
HathiTrust

women's novels, its initial edition contains no illustrations or cover art. Much of the narrative's focus is on Ellen becoming a good Christian, as taught first by her mother, and then by her friends, the Humphreys, after her mother dies. Alongside this religious training, Ellen tends to the sick, including her mother, her cruel Aunt Fortune, and her friend, Alice Humphrey. It is no coincidence that Ellen's Christianity corresponds with her care for others, as nineteenth-century Christian leaders, such as Horace Bushnell, collapse the two, noting that a mother's care of a child is akin to the care Christ shows.[179] When Ellen is sent to live with her Scottish relatives, Ellen refuses to renounce her American heritage and her religious beliefs, with her Americanness being absorbed into her feminine identity. The text rewards this behavior, and Ellen eventually returns to the United States as John Humphrey's wife, proving that her rebellion, slight as it is, actually cements her place in the American cult of domesticity.

The eponymous protagonist of Susan Coolidge's *What Katy Did* (1872) is a sharp contrast to Ellen. Some might classify the novel as a family story, given that her siblings feature prominently in the novel. However, the story centers on the motherless Katy, as she is raised by her father and Aunt Izzie, who like Rebecca's Aunt Miranda and Pollyanna's Aunt Polly, is unable to relate to Katy. A tomboy, Katy is more apt to start a physically rough game with her siblings than to sit quietly. For example, Aunt Izzie finds that Katy's bonnet string is pinned instead of sewn. As Aunt Izzie sews it on, lecturing Katy in the process, Katy fidgets, "uttering a little snort, like an impatient horse" and "[t]he minute she was released she flew into the kitchen ... and rushed like a whirlwind to the gate, where good little Clover stood patiently waiting."[180] Katy is in sharp contrast to her "good" sister, who is ready for school, presumably with a properly sewn string. Bonnets, as noted throughout girls' literature, are a mark of femininity, preserving one's (often white) complexion and limiting a girl's vision, like horses' blinders. Notably, Katy has not sewn a *bonnet* to Aunt Izzie's satisfaction. In this passage, Katy is compared to a horse and a whirlwind,

[179] Douglas, *The Feminization of American Culture*, p. 128.
[180] Coolidge, *Katy*, p. 25.

wild parts of nature. This comparison correlates with Gina M. Dorré's argument that "the problems wrought by ... domestic ideology" can be mapped onto "the cultural practice of horsebreaking."[181] More specifically, the so-called broken horse symbolically is "recast in female form – guided by nature, gentled to duty."[182] These words could be used to describe Katy's domestication: gentled through illness, she eventually assumes her feminine duty without resistance.

Katy famously disobeys her aunt and falls off a broken swing, becoming paralyzed for the next four years, during which time her disposition changes. Katy's illness springs out of her disobedience, as well as her physical activity, which Elizabeth Hale notes has a sexual undercurrent.[183] In contrast, Cousin Helen serves as the angelic figure, whose lack of physical presence (she is also paralyzed) reinforces her noncarnal nature. Cousin Helen fulfills the role of othermother and helps guide Katy to running the household, mothering her siblings, and becoming less physically present (quite literally caring "from above" in her upstairs bedroom). Noble notes the literary connection between restricted femininity and absence: that a true woman "was trained to behave in such a way as to suggest her own physical absence."[184] Katy's inner transformation leads to a physical one, and by the novel's end, Katy can walk again. Now she prioritizes quiet femininity over moving like a whirlwind. Cousin Helen observes Katy's conversion into what she calls the "Heart of the House": "the gentle expression of her eyes, the womanly look, the pleasant voice, the politeness, the tact in advising the others, without seeming to advise."[185] The illustrations capture this change, with the frontispiece showing Katy leading her siblings and friend outside in nature (Figure 15), and the final illustration depicting

---

[181] G. M. Dorré, *Victorian Fiction and the Cult of the Horse* (Abingdon: Ashgate, 2006), p. 65.

[182] Ibid., p. 66.

[183] E. Hale, "Disability and the individual talent: Adolescent girlhood in *The Pillars of the House* and *What Katy Did*," *Women's Writing*, 17.2 (2010), 343–360, p. 352.

[184] Noble, *Masochistic Pleasures*, p. 35. [185] Coolidge, *Katy*, pp. 219, 218.

ENTERING PARADISE. — Page 23.

So in they marched, Katy and Cecy heading the procession, and Dorry, with his great trailing bunch of boughs, bringing up the rear.

Figure 15 Susan Coolidge, *What Katy Did* (1872), frontispiece – HathiTrust

Katy in bed, surrounding by her siblings at Christmas (Figure 16). These two images contrast, in one Katy's domain is outside, and she holds a position of authority. In the second, Katy is immobile, the "heart of the house," with little agency. Katy's presence, after having been literally

" How perfectly lovely everybody is," said Katy, with grateful tears in her
eyes. — PAGE 203.

Figure 16 Susan Coolidge, *What Katy Did* (1872), np – HathiTrust

erased by her confinement, is now willingly made smaller, as she adheres to what Claudia Nelson terms "Katy's perfect conformity to the nineteenth-century domestic novel's archetype of virtue."[186]

While many of these orphan stories feature heroines who must adapt to a demure femininity, sometimes, the transformation is slightly more radical. Bestselling author Dorothy Canfield (later Canfield Fisher) wrote such a heroine. Notably, Canfield helped influence the American literary marketplace in the 1920s and 30s, as one of the five judges who selected the Book-of-the-Month Club, which, in 1929, had over 110,000 subscribers.[187] Her support of Maria Montessori's educational methods and of "traditional values"[188] can be seen in *Understood Betsy* (1916). The eponymous heroine, who until nine years old was raised by a nervous, kindhearted cousin named Frances, and consequently, Betsy is timid. In true Montessori fashion, the text touts the benefit of leaving a child alone, as Frances's attempts to "thoroughly understand [Betsy] down to the bottom of her little mind" cause more harm than good.[189] When Frances leaves Betsy with her New England relatives, they expect independence from Betsy. Suddenly, she must walk to school alone, complete chores, and even care for a younger girl. In this sense, Betsy has little influence on her family, other than serving as the typical childhood "light in the home," brightening up their daily lives. Instead, Betsy spends the novel conforming to the girlhood her family prefers, which uniquely requires more agency than is typical of contemporary fictional girls. Ada C. Williamson's illustrations capture Betsy's newfound agency: talking and acting alone (Figure 17). Yet, Betsy's overall role is still confined to the feminine realm, as she cooks, cleans, and cares for others.

A bookend of sorts is the Newbery Award-winning *Roller Skates* (1936) by Ruth Sawyer. Much like the *Betsy-Tacy* and *Little House* series, the book

---

[186] C. Nelson, "What Katy read: Susan Coolidge and the image of the Victorian child," *Children's Literature Quarterly*, 1991 Proceedings, 217–22, p. 221.
[187] J. A. Radway, *A Feeling for Books: The Book-of-the-Month Club, Literary Taste, and Middle-Class Desire* (Chapel Hill: University of North Carolina Press, 1997), pp. 178, 261.
[188] Ibid., p. 178. [189] Canfield, *Betsy*, p. 4.

Betsy shut her teeth together hard, and started across.

Figure 17 Dorothy Canfield, *Understood Betsy* (New York, 1916), np –
HathiTrust

was written in the 1930s, but set in the 1890s. In it, Lucinda, the youngest child in an upper-class family, becomes a temporary orphan for a year, while her parents holiday abroad. The text creates a juxtaposition between the family and orphan girls' stories, acknowledging the orphan heroine's freedom. In spite of her mother's influence, Lucinda is "not pretty, given to tantrums, to be disciplined and endured."[190] Lucinda's Aunt Emily requires quiet, ladylike behavior, to the point that her husband nicknames their four daughters the "gazelles,"[191] presumably because they are quiet, graceful, and indistinguishable, the opposite of Lucinda.

The push and pull of Emily's domestic influence and Lucinda's newfound freedom come to conflict during Lucinda's orphanhood. When Emily criticizes Lucinda's sewing, Lucinda's temper bursts forth: "The whole Fourth of July went off inside of Lucinda. Her sewing basket, scissors, thimble, work went across the room."[192] Lucinda rejects sewing, the metaphorical hallmark of femininity. Her rage is compared to the fireworks at American Independence Day, and independence is exactly what Lucinda gets after this incident. Her outburst of anger, while not exactly condoned, never results in punishment. Instead, her uncle Earle intervenes, taking her up to the library (his own quarters), and introducing her to the works of William Shakespeare. She never sews with her aunt and cousins again; instead, she spends her Saturday afternoons reading Shakespeare with her uncle. Shakespeare is often coded feminine in this period;[193] nevertheless, the plays contrast the *Elsie Dinsmore* books Emily's daughters read. Lucinda's temper frees her to participate in a more "masculine" space.

Similarly, the text emphasizes the roller skates that Lucinda uses for transportation: the cover depicts her skating. Skates are both representative of and the actual key to her mobility in the city. Her guardians give her few rules, and Emily becomes less influential. In her orphanhood, Lucinda befriends Italian immigrants. She teaches English to a woman who may be

---

[190] Sawyer, *Skates*, p. 173. [191] Ibid., p. 72. [192] Sawyer, *Skates*, p. 52.
[193] "Tales from Shakespeare" is behind the Bible in a list of books every girl should own (A. Preston, "The girl who is starting a library: Some of the books she should have," *Ladies' Home Journal*, 23.12 [1906], p. 34).

from the Middle East (the text is unclear, using Turkish and oriental to describe the woman and her belongings). Lucinda also becomes acquainted and dines with an Irish cab driver and his wife. The emphasis on immigrants and the intermingling of the upper, middle, and lower classes, makes this book unusual for girls' literature. Uncle Earle tells Lucinda that this year will save her from "Snobbishness – priggishness – the Social Register."[194] The novel implies that this year of orphanhood, or freedom, is temporary, but, as Uncle Earle suggests, will have a lasting impact on Lucinda. It becomes an orphan novel in reverse in this way. Lucinda has always desired for independence, but not until she is "orphaned" can she act on it. Thus, her return to society will not be "normal," in spite of her parents' best efforts.

Sawyer's sequel, *The Year of Jubilo* (1940),[195] depicts a rather different ending for Lucinda. After Lucinda's father's death, the family, including Lucinda's three older brothers, moves to a house in Maine. Early in the novel, an older brother recommends she "make allowances" for another brother's cruelty.[196] He then paints a picture of womanhood that rivals Coventry Patmore's iconic *The Angel in the House* (1854):

> [Women] know mercy, they know compassion, they know forgiveness in a measure that is far beyond a man's compass ... You can stay a fighting, disagreeable hoyden, or you can grow in understanding, in lovely ways, in a gentle giving-in that won't hurt you.[197]

For the rest of the novel, Lucinda strives to live up to her brother's ideal. Gone is Lucinda the roller skater, who throws tantrums and chooses Shakespeare over sewing. In spite of the ninety-year age gap between this book and *The Wide, Wide World*, Lucinda's written fate is not much different from Ellen's. Like the other female orphans in this section, once united (or in this case reunited) with a family, Lucinda is expected to adhere to a certain role, one in which compassion for others erases her natural

---

[194] Sawyer, *Skates*, p. 78.
[195] R. Sawyer, *The Year of Jubilo* (New York: Viking Press, 1940).
[196] Ibid., p. 24.   [197] Ibid., p. 25.

inclinations, and tantrums are but a faded memory, replaced with more restricted speech. Orphaned heroines must "grow down" in growing up.

Each of these orphans in some ways demonstrates agency, but that freedom is restricted to their girlhood. The fate (implied or depicted) for each of them is marriage, keeping the publication history of girls' novels socially conservative. This domestic ending, however, is not the only option for schoolgirls' stories.

5 "Vassar Graduates Do Marry": School Stories

Girls' schools offer a girls' only space in which to pursue scholastics, as well as athletics and leadership positions, novel opportunities in the late nineteenth century. Girls' boarding schools appeared in the early nineteenth century, and women's colleges were established thereafter, with 1880–1910 considered the latter's "golden age."[198] Publishers quickly capitalized on this trend, resulting in the girls' school story. While school settings are often part of both family and orphan stories, and even women's literature (cf. Follen's *Sketches of my Schoolmates*), the novels in this subgenre *center* around the educational setting. This subgenre was popular, especially in the early twentieth century: "The number of school and college stories advertised in the back pages of such books as the *Marjorie Dean* series [1917–25] reflect a growing and continuous consumer demand."[199] Book historian John Tebbel lists Jean Webster's college novel *Daddy Long Legs* (1912) as one "of the most popular novels of the day."[200] In addition to reflecting a real-world experience, these texts feature heroines with high levels of agency, arguably contributing to their popularity.

Certain opportunities are unique to the school story, in part because of the characters' privileged social status. These real-life schools were expensive, resulting in mostly wealthy white students. Consequently, school stories also feature fairly homogeneous, privileged characters, which lends some permissiveness towards their misbehavior. There are specific boundaries: these behaviors are restricted to the school space. For this reason, the school becomes almost magical, where girls are able to extend the freedom associated with childhood, postponing their inevitable entrance into the cult of domesticity. Shirley Marchalonis calls this location-based suspension the "green world" of college, a place with "its own rules; it offered women more room to define themselves than they could find anywhere else."[201] In this section,

---

[198] S. A. Inness, *Intimate Communities: Representation and Social Transformation in Women's College Fiction, 1895–1910* (Bowling Green, OH: Bowling Green State University Popular Press), p. 1.

[199] Rosoff and Spencer, *School Stories*, pp. 4–5.   [200] Tebbel, Vol. II, p. 372.

[201] S. Marchalonis, *College Girls: A Century in Fiction* (Rutgers University Press, 1995), p. 4.

I apply Marchalonis' definition to boarding schools as well, noting that these school settings also exist as a liminal environment in which girls can behave outside of societal expectations. This so-called magical space offers girls the chance to be and do more than they could at home, such as compete in athletics, participate in school government, and develop romantic female friendships, known as "crushes." It is too radical to say that the protagonist with a college degree officially grows "up," although one could argue that Pratt's growing down[202] is suspended for those four years and occasionally beyond, extending the freedoms of girlhood into young adulthood. Women's colleges had the potential to challenge the accepted, even celebrated roles of wife and mother offered to women.

The early books in the subgenre acknowledge the opportunities for college graduates. In Lizzie Champney's 1885 *Three Vassar Girls in South America*, one character observes: "[T]here are more resources for single women nowadays than formerly. They can do more, and can enjoy all the privileges of the age, as well as their married sisters."[203] In reality, between the 1870s and 1920s, "between 40 and 60 percent of women college graduates did not marry, at a time when only 10 percent of American women did not."[204] However, around the 1890s, colleges began to overtly assure the public that female graduates are "choosing marriage and domesticity over a career and independence."[205] Girls' school stories have a similar trajectory. Some early novels, such as *Vassar Girls*, portray career opportunities, but most texts assure readers that educated women are more capable domestically because of their time at college. The real-life, and therefore fictional, curriculum resembled men's colleges, with "subjects as geography, history, grammar, physiology, chemistry, theology, astronomy,

---

[202] Pratt, *Archetypal Patterns*, p. 30.

[203] L. W. Champney, *Three Vassar Girls in South America. A Holiday Trip of Three College Girls through the Southern Continent, Up the Amazon, Down the Madeira, Across the Andes, and Up the Pacific Coast to Panama* (Boston, MA: Estes and Lauriat, 1885), p. 238.

[204] Carroll Smith-Rosenberg, *Disorderly Conduct: Visions of Gender in Victorian America* (New York: A.A. Knopf, 1985), p. 253.

[205] Inness, *Intimate Communities*, pp. 7–8.

rhetoric, and philosophy."[206] Arguably, then the socialization of college is what prepares heroines for the cult of domesticity, to set aside their identities as students, athletes, and crushes, in favor of the communal identities of mothers and wives. The "privilege" *Vassar Girls* identifies is quelled as the subgenre matures, leading to the eventual replacement of the college setting with high school in the 1930s.

In this section, I first highlight the opportunities offered in the green space. These stories' implicit adherence to social standards becomes more overt than with orphan characters. I explore the use of the school community to prepare the girl for marriage, mirroring the socialization an adoptive family might have supplied in orphan novels. Then the final section develops the tension between the careers alluded to in early novels and the conventional marital endings that inevitably happened in most texts, resembling the real-world colleges' assurance that their graduates maintain their femininity alongside their bachelor's degrees.

The ten novels examined in this section have six publishers. As in previous sections, there is a consistent tie between author and publisher. Jean Webster's four school novels were published by The Century Company, and Margaret Warde's two series by Penn Publishing. The notable exception is A. L. Burt, known for its series fiction, which published Pauline Lester's *Marjorie Dean* series[207] and Harriet Pyne Grove's *Betty Lee* series.[208] Series fiction remains prominent in this girls' subgenre. All of the books in this section have at least one sequel, with many series extending into four or more books, giving readers the opportunity to follow the heroine through each year of school and sometimes beyond. The novels examined in this section were published between 1883 and 1931, framing women's colleges' "golden age," and are set at either a boarding school or women's college.

5.1 Green Space of Boarding School and College

Boarding schools and colleges place the protagonist in an all-female community, lacking direct parental supervision, and thus supplying

---

[206] Rosoff and Spencer, *School Stories*, p. 71.

[207] P. Lester, *Marjorie Dean* series (New York: A.L. Burt, 1917–25).

[208] H. P. Grove, *Betty Lee* series (New York: A.L. Burt, 1931).

more freedom than at home. A character from Margaret Warde's *Nancy Lee* (1912) observes: "Why shouldn't girls act sensible at boarding-school as well as at other places? ... You wouldn't think of doing such silly things anywhere else."[209] This absence of gender-based decorum underpins girls' school stories: in the "green world" societal rules are somewhat suspended. Notably, the narrative rarely depicts what happens in the classroom; instead, the focus is female friendships, which develop in social spaces, such as dormitories or common areas. Rosoff and Spencer argue that the "significance of these spaces [provides] for the informal learning of fictional characters."[210] Thus, the stories are less about academics, and more about the community-based socialization. The girls' agency is increased, as the story occurs where they have the highest authority.

In these stories, girls follow teachers' rules only so long as these strictures serve the female community; for example, most texts feature a "lights out" rule designating when to sleep. However, the evening is ideal for socialization and thus, girls co-opt this time for domestic feasts called "spreads," what Sardella-Ayres refers to as "a type of female-centric communion."[211] Here, the girls subvert the domestic art of cooking by making and eating school-specific delicacies, such as fudge and rarebit (cheese sauce on toast). They utilize a chafing dish, which upper- and middle-class women use for warming, not cooking, food. Preparing the meal takes place in front of and often incorporates the guests, a taboo in refined society. More than that, the food is "consumed in the bedroom," which Inness views as "socially transgressive."[212] As the majority of these girls are wealthy, cooking while a gendered task, was often assigned to a servant. Thus, the spread goes beyond defying the school authority, and becomes a sort of defiance against the upper class and the cult of domesticity

---

[209] M. Warde, *Nancy Lee* (Philadelphia: Penn Publishing, 1912), pp. 252–3.

[210] Rosoff and Spencer, *School Stories*, p. 61.

[211] D. Sardella-Ayres, "Food and community in American college girl fiction," *FEAST Journal: Consuming Children*, 1 (2018), n.p.

[212] Inness, *Intimate Communities*, p. 38.

This somewhat layered rebellion occurs throughout these stories, from Helen Dawes Brown's *Two College Girls* (1886),[213] one of the first college novels, to the 1922 *Marjorie Dean, College Freshman*, wherein the frontispiece illustration depicts a spread (Figure 18). Food becomes a way for college girls to foster an all-female community; nevertheless, their families' unspoken influence remains, as privilege underscores this somewhat defiant behavior. Also present is their future familial duty: "College fiction does not contest the cultural assumption that college women must eventually make the progression from cooking for a group of friends to cooking for a - family."[214] Thus, even these transgressive behaviors prepare girls for their future domestic roles.

These novels also feature "crushes," wherein typically younger girls somewhat romantically pursue an older student. In *Betty Wales, Freshman* (1906), a crush is defined as "a warm and adoring friendship."[215] This friendship involves "displays of affection such as gift giving, poetry writing to the beloved, and often frequent kissing and hugging."[216] These relationships are viewed positively in the texts, with only a few exceptions. For example, Nancy Lee finds "crushes ... awfully silly."[217] Arguably, Nancy's opinion serves as censure against the selfish Vera, the younger girls' crush, rather than the practice. Another negative viewpoint is that of Edna Howe in Brown's *Two College Girls*. While there are no crushes per se, open affection occurs frequently. The plot centers on two heroines becoming well-rounded girls: Edna grows socially and Rosemary scholastically. Unsurprising, the socially unsure Edna at first finds Rosemary's kissing "superfluous and embarrassing."[218] As J. Hillis Miller notes, even when given platonically, a "kiss always has an erotic dimension,"[219] which perhaps explains why Edna shies away from Rosemary's affection. Kisses

---

[213] H. D. Brown, *Two College Girls* (Boston, MA: Houghton, Mifflin, 1886).

[214] Inness, *Intimate Communities*, p. 38.

[215] M. Warde, *Betty Wales, Freshman* (Philadelphia: Penn Publishing, 1906), p. 47.

[216] Inness, *Intimate Communities*, p. 47. [217] Warde, *Nancy Lee*, p. 57.

[218] Brown, *Two College Girls*, p. 47.

[219] J. H. Miller, "What is a kiss? Isabel's moment of decision," *Critical Inquiry*, 31.3 (2005), 722–46, p. 725.

The next day's recitations hastily prepared, the
Lookouts had gathered in Ronny's room for a spread.
(*Marjorie Dean, College Freshman*)   *Page 207*

Figure 18 Pauline Lester, *Marjorie Dean*, *College Freshman* (New York, 1922), frontispiece – HathiTrust

between friends, particularly among the upper classes, are not unusual, and working-class Edna is unaccustomed to many of her peer group's behaviors. Edna learns to dissociate the kiss from sexual connotations, as indeed the text does, and welcomes Rosemary's kisses.[220] This change in Edna proves her proper assimilation into college life and her peers' social class.

Modern readers might detect a homoerotic subtext, but crushes are not meant to be sexual.[221] Instead, they are a vehicle for older girls to mentor younger ones in the female community.[222] In *Betty Wales, Freshman*, Betty idolizes junior Dorothy, who helps Betty through her first year. In *Nancy Lee*, the character of Kittie has a similar, albeit more negative, experience with her crush, Vera. When Kittie missteps socially, Vera reprimands and punishes her. Bestowing romantic affection on a student may appear subversive, but, as with many school exceptions, the crush is limited to school. The green world permits romance between girls, so long as it leads to heterosexual marriage.

In addition to hosting spreads and having crushes, the school-story heroine is often more mischievous than those in family or orphan stories, or, perhaps more accurately, she is more intentionally mischievous. Some characters, such as Brown's Rosamond or Warde's Nancy, amend their behavior over the course of the novel or series, creating a moral arc. However, one protagonist remains the same, making her an important exception in this subgenre. Webster's Patty, from *When Patty Went to College* (1903)[223] and *Just Patty* (1911), excels "in impudence and audacity."[224] In the first *Patty* novel, as a senior at college,[225] Patty has a reputation for causing harmless trouble. For example, Patty decorates her room in direct opposition to the school's policy, and the janitor who initially scolds Patty, eventually installs her banned stove. Patty avoids punishment and is aided by someone who should report her. This occurrence is important enough to be depicted in one of the novel's six illustrations

[220] Brown, *Two College Girls*, p. 283. [221] Inness, *Intimate Communities*, p. 47.

[222] Ibid., p. 46.

[223] J. Webster, *When Patty Went to College* (New York: Century Company, 1903).

[224] J. Webster, *Just Patty* (New York: Century Company, 1911), p. 35.

[225] *Just Patty* covers Patty's time at boarding school, before college.

(Figure 19). In it, Patty stands on a ladder clearly "above" the janitor. She looks almost coyly at the viewer, while the janitor looks at her. The caption reads: "Men know such a lot about such things!"[226] However, Patty's expression reveals the truth: she is manipulating this situation. This event is representative of Patty's mischief: for the most part, no one gets hurt, but Patty continually has the upper hand.

As with many of these college girls' story heroines, the text makes it clear that Patty is ultimately "good." Her moral behavior is measured by its effect on the female community. At one point, Patty feigns illness in order to study, but when the professor remarks: "I should not ask you to take the examination at all if I thought it would be fair to the rest of the class," Patty confesses and requests a mark of zero for the exam.[227] Patty acts, not out of respect for authority, but fairness to her peers. Her decision mirrors the justification for after-hours spreads, prioritizing community-building in the green world.

Of course, a certain level of privilege underscores Patty's conduct. These heroines may "deal in subterfuges and evasions,"[228] but "still manage to affirm the basic values of their class and gender."[229] Patty acknowledges the feminine society she must enter on graduation, but the novel ends on a more uncertain note. When the bishop confronts Patty about her reputation, Patty confesses her final crime to the female student president. While a chastisement from the patriarchal representative, the bishop, affects Patty, its permanence is doubtful. After her confession, Patty remarks: "I may think of some good excuse [to avoid punishment] in the night."[230] Patty's amended behavior may not last, neither is she engaged to be married, ready to submit to the cult of domesticity. With the novel ending right before graduation, Patty remains suspended in the green world. Ultimately, the green world is an illusion of freedom, as the all-female community serves to socialize heroines, preparing them for the upper-class domesticity for which they are destined. This trajectory becomes apparent in school stories featuring orphans.

---

[226] Ibid. [227] Ibid., pp. 118–19. [228] Webster, *Patty Went to College*, p. 279.
[229] Stoneley, *Consumerism and American Girls' Literature*, p. 78.
[230] Webster, *Patty Went to College*, p. 277.

Men know such a lot about such things!

Figure 19 Jean Webster, *Patty Went to College* (New York, 1903), np – HathiTrust

5.2 The Orphan Heroine

While we might think of school as a space in which girls claim agency, as Inness observes: "In this isolated women's community, economics are never far beneath the surface: the parents who pay for the education or the spread are always present, even if they are not frequently portrayed."[231] This observation of families as ever-present background figures connects to the difference between what I term "family heroines" and orphan heroines. The majority of the protagonists discussed in this section have a family, and, importantly, a mother. Just as sections 3 and 4 observe that an orphaned heroine has more freedom, but fewer social advantages than the family protagonist, so there are notable differences for orphans in school stories.

Orphan girls often begin the novels outside society, having grown up without a family, particularly a mother, to guide them into proper girlhood. The orphan's *entwicklungsroman* comprises the orphan assimilating into society, becoming less "odd" and more in line with societal expectations for women. When the orphan is arguably already an adult, a husband becomes the family she seeks. In Webster's epistolary novel *Daddy Long Legs*, an orphaned Judy enters college aware that she exists outside societal boundaries, that she is unlike other girls. She bemoans that: "The things that most girls with a properly assorted family and a home and friends and a library know by absorption, I have never heard of."[232] This knowledge comprises the social markers of middle- and upper-class, white womanhood. Without a mother to teach her, the other college girls fill this role, assimilating Judy into society, preparing her for the cult of domesticity. As Stoneley observes: "Vassar does not turn [Judy] into a lawyer or a doctor, so much as make her more marriageable."[233] Thus, Judy's education is about learning domesticity, more than scholastic achievement.

A similar occurrence happens with Lloyd in Warde's *Nancy Lee*. She has a father, but no mother, and her resulting behavior makes her an outsider at school. Her roommate Kittie describes her as "big and terribly tanned and awkward. Wore her hair skinned straight back, and her clothes look as if

---

[231] Inness, *Intimate Communities*, p. 42. [232] Ibid., p. 46.
[233] Stoneley, *Consumerism and American Girls' Literature*, p. 15.

they came out of the Ark."[234] Like Judy, Lloyd is unaware of the fashion and social graces that her peers learned from their mothers. Her time spent outside riding horses has "tanned" her skin, further alienating her from the idealized femininity of "slim, pale, passive beings."[235] However, following the trend in school stories, Lloyd's "muscular physique and athletic vigor are considered desirable traits."[236] As with Judy, Lloyd's classmates will now form a collective mother, bringing Lloyd into the social fold.

This socialization underpins Edith Bancroft's *Jane Allen of the Sub-Team* (1917).[237] Motherless Jane grew up in Montana, where her father allowed her to roam freely on horseback, unrestricted by social mores. Like Lloyd, Jane must go east to be "tamed." Jane's "battle against self"[238] is to assimilate with her peers. She arrives at college with little knowledge of the social rules that govern college life. In addition to her peers' influence, the institution, called "mother" in the college anthem, socializes Jane. Jane frequently turns to her deceased mother for guidance. At the novel's turning point, Jane pledges to embrace college life to both "mothers": "Dear Mother in Heaven, and dear Alma Mater, for the sake of one who loved me and the other Mother whose child I hope to be, I'll begin all over again and try to do my best!"[239] Her vow succeeds, as she ends the novel with loyal friends, having learned to value the female community.

While Lloyd and Jane are wealthy, other orphans are not. *Daddy Long Legs'* Judy is sent to college to write, and through hard work and what Avery terms orphan virtue,[240] Judy establishes herself as an author. However, her story follows a fairy tale arc when she marries her benefactor in a rags-to-riches ending. Like the heroines in orphan girls' stories, Judy must succumb to societal expectations for women. Whereas in *Daddy Long Legs*, Judy writes the letters and is therefore the narrator, in the sequel *Dear Enemy* (1915),[241]

---

[234] Warde, *Nancy Lee*, p. 15.

[235] Gilbert and Gubar, *Madwoman in the Attic*, p. 25.

[236] Inness, *Intimate Communities*, p. 82.

[237] E. Bancroft, *Jane Allen of the Sub-Team* (Akron, OH: Saalfield Publishing, 1917).

[238] Ibid., p. 194. [239] Ibid., p. 70. [240] Avery, *Behold the Child*, p. 179.

[241] J. Webster, *Dear Enemy* (New York: Century Company, 1915).

Judy receives the letters. Instead of having agency through narration, Judy is now a wife and mother, with no mention of her writing. This absence recalls the pen and penis similarities drawn by Gilbert and Gubar, in that, in the patriarchy, both are "instrument[s] of generative power."[242] As a married woman, Judy no longer lays claim to such power. She is silenced, as even the letters she writes are excluded from the text. We can only guess at what her pen has generated, by reading the unmarried (and therefore still empowered) narrator's letters. Instead, Judy maintains "a happy picture of domestic concord."[243] *Dear Enemy* does not fit the college girls' model, but neither does Judy. As a part of a successful orphan story arc, Judy has moved from college to the home and as a result, is now fulfilled by "marriage and motherhood,"[244] not writing. This trajectory is notable coming from a female author. Webster died soon after her marriage, so whether she would have followed Judy's path is unknown. However, female authors denied their heroines writing careers, as perhaps most famously demonstrated by Jo March in *Little Women*.[245] Jo's future was determined by Alcott's publisher and readers who wanted Jo to marry,[246] markedly dividing the real-world female authors' and their fictional heroines' opportunities. Judy, along with Lloyd and Jane, demonstrate that the orphan's goal of fitting into society can, and must, be met in the school setting.

5.3 Marriage or Career?

The tension between the green space and the expected femininity is at play throughout the school story subgenre. As demonstrated above, school stories generally portray the heroine's socialization into the cult of domesticity; however, earlier novels offered heroines a different *bildungsroman* trajectory: a career. For example, Champney's *Three Vassar Girls Abroad*[247]

---

[242] Gilbert and Gubar, *Madwoman in the* Attic, p. 6.

[243] Webster, *Dear Enemy*, p. 121. [244] Baym, *Woman's Fiction*, p. 26.

[245] Jo eventually resumes writing in *Jo's Boys* (1886).

[246] Foster and Simons, *What Katy Read*, p. 92.

[247] L. W. Champney. *Three Vassar Girls Abroad: Rambles of Three College Girls on a Vacation Trip through France and Spain for Amusement and Instruction* (Boston, MA: Estes and Lauriat, 1883).

features a remarkably different opinion of marriage. When Barbara expresses a romantic opinion, her friend, Maud, chastises her, claiming she is "a Vassar girl." However, Barbara stands by her romantic notions, observing that "Vassar graduates do marry" and that she will be one of them: "I am going to make the very most of my education and of my opportunities . . . in order to be worthy of some good man's love."[248] Her speech argues an education can support not hinder preparation for the cult of domesticity, better suiting her to be her husband's helpmate.

However, more striking is Maud's assertion that when alumna bring their husbands to events, the sight "console[s] all the old maids." While the text does not elaborate on what makes these husbands undesirable, what is clear is Maud's belief that no husband is worth the sacrifice of independence. Whether the reader is supposed to sympathize with Barbara or Maud is unknown, but notably, both opinions are allowed to coexist. Should Maud have changed her mind after Barbara's speech, we might assume the text's underpinning ideology promotes a more conservative approach to education and marriage. However, Maud remains steadfast in her determination to stay unmarried and pursue art, in contrast to most of the other texts examined in this Element.

In Brown's 1886 *Two College Girls*, the two heroines and their friends discuss their futures. One declares that "[i]f I were a man, I should not have the least respect for a woman that couldn't have had a destiny of her own if I'd never existed"; another retorts, albeit "boldly," that she "believe[s] in every woman's being married."[249] These supposedly competing ideas of either having a destined career or marriage play out in the two protagonists. The novel ends with Rosamond on the path to become a doctor, with no plans to marry, although she hopes that she might someday. In contrast, Edna is engaged to be married, but there is a tension here between Edna's independence and education. While she is permitted to work for now, when they marry her focus must become her husband. When he proposes, he references a speech she gave, asking Edna to "keep me . . . feeling [inspired]."[250] His request requires her to transition from inspiring crowds to only inspiring him. This offer is akin to what Anne Scott MacLeod calls

[248] Ibid., p. 123. [249] Brown, *Two College Girls*, p. 289. [250] Ibid., p. 324.

"the bargain offered nineteenth-century women: influence in exchange for freedom; a role as 'inspiration' in place of real power."[251] The exchange of freedom for supposed influence, which was so pervasive in early American women's literature, exists in a college novel fifty years later. In spite of her scholastic achievements, Edna will teach for only a few years, and then she must grow down and inspire her husband.

As with the majority of girls' fiction in this Element, heroines, even precocious, college-educated heroines, are expected to become wives and mothers in the vein of domesticity. Inness observes, college fiction "does not challenge the status quo of the outside world; instead, women's college graduates are trained to adjust themselves to their new situation and recognize that the college years must be only a fond memory for any woman who has successfully matured."[252] In this vein, readers learn of Maud's engagement in a *Vassar Girls* sequel. Maud's reputation causes a student to exclaim: "I never would have believed it of her; she is so downright sensible, and a Vassar girl too."[253] Thus, Inness' assertions of the temporary nature of the independence and agency of college are outlined even in this early series. The characters' continued expectation that Vassar graduates will maintain their independence points to a future beyond the cult of domesticity for the girls' heroine. In many ways, this sentiment is the promise of the green world of the girls' school story.

This subgenre ultimately aligns with the limited *bildungsroman* that defines the overarching girls' literature genre. As time progresses, school stories double down their commitment to a more conservative ending. School stories shift to the high school setting, mirroring a societal shift. American society of the 1930s for the most part viewed attending a women's college as restricting and even harmful (as crushes are viewed as precursors to lesbianism), and coeducational college were rarely welcoming to female students. As a result, school stories changed as well, with "narratives of the women's colleges published around 1930" depicting colleges as "agents of destruction."[254] The replacement high school

---

[251] MacLeod, *American Childhood*, p. 4.   [252] Inness, *Intimate Communities*, p. 109.
[253] Champney, *Vassar Girls in South America*, p. 238.
[254] Marchalonis, *College Girls*, p. 127.

novels, like Harriet Pyne Grove's *Betty Lee* series (1931), almost always end in marriage or the promise of marriage. As education became more widely available to real-life girls, the published novels actively encourage their readers to settle for the safety of domesticity, after a few scholastic adventures, of course.

6 "This is What Our Race Needs": African American Girls' Literature

The previous sections have examined literature depicting a specific girl: one who is white, middle to upper class, Protestant, cis-gendered, and heterosexual, following the "common trope of constructing childhood [in this case, girlhood] as white."[255] This section attempts to complicate the publishing histories of the nineteenth and early twentieth centuries, which, by and large, reflect the cultural silencing of nonwhite heroines. In analyzing American girls' literature, the conversation must include other voices. As Dianne Johnson observes, "when considering American children's literature, the critic must recognize that there is not, definitively, one national mythology. There is a 'White' one and an African American one, at the crudest level."[256] While this Element's focus is not necessarily American mythology, Johnson's argument for a dual approach to American children's literature (that is multiplied as we incorporate other identities), is another reason to incorporate the book history of African American girls' literature.[257]

As noted in section 1, labelling this genre as African American girls' literature is problematic, as it essentially "Othered" nonwhite heroines and/ or fiction written for an implied nonwhite reader. African American girls' fiction does not function as a subgenre of girls' literature, as these books include the range of subgenres explored in the previous sections. There are African American orphan, family, and school stories. Simply acknowledging this dynamic does not solve the problem but hopefully invites dialogue.

This Element, in defining girls' literature as a genre, uses certain qualities to determine appropriate books: being a novel, having a publication date between 1850 and 1940, written by a woman, published

---

[255] B. Fielder, "Black girls, white girls, American girls: Slavery and racialized perspectives in abolitionist and neoabolistionist children's literature," *Tulsa Studies in Women's Literature*, 36.2 (2017), 323–52, p. 325.

[256] D. Johnson, *Telling Tales: The Pedagogy and Promise of African American Literature for Youth* (Westport, CT: Greenwood Press, 1990), p. 7.

[257] The use of "African American" refers to people of African descent in the United States. (Fielder, 'Black girls, white girls, American girls', p. 348, n. 7).

and set in the United States, and falling into the broader genre of domestic realism. These same boundaries apply to the texts examined in this section; however, there are some limitations, accounting for the prolonged emergence of published books written about and for African American girls. This section examines some of the first published novels written by African American authors. One was originally published as a serialization in an African American newspaper. The other two were published by a religious press, the American Baptist Publication Society. Finally, the last section bends the parameters by examining short stories from W. E. B. DuBois' children's periodical, *The Brownies' Book.*[258]

In the last few decades, several African American female authors' works were recovered; however, these novels often address mature topics, such as slavery, rape, and abuse, which traditionally are not considered appropriate for child readers, and therefore, not children's literature. As a result, I have excluded these texts from this section, defining girls' literature in part by its audience. However, in making this choice, I limit what might be considered African American girls' literature. Scholars such as Robin Bernstein observe that African American girlhood is not socially constructed as "innocently" as white girlhood is,[259] thus making a text like Frances E. W. Harper's *Iola Leroy, or Shadows Uplifted* (1892),[260] a novel about a mixed-race girl who is captured and enslaved, a potentially valid inclusion, although one I have intentionally left out of my corpus.

Instead, I have chosen books that sometimes have dual/multiple protagonists and, as noted below, the protagonists' race is sometimes in question. Mainstream publishing featured white woman authors' representations of African American girls, which are generally problematic, as their portrayals are stereotypical at best. However, this authorship is unsurprising in terms of African American children's literature generally. Rudine Sims Bishop observes that "[w]ithin the context of American children's literature, Black

---

[258] J. R. Fauset (ed.), *The Brownies' Book* (New York: DuBois & Dill, 1920–1).

[259] R. Bernstein, *Racial Innocence: Performing American Childhood from Slavery to Civil Rights* (New York: New York University Press, 2011).

[260] F. E. W. Harper, *Iola Leroy, or Shadows Uplifted* (New York: Penguin Classics, 2010; original 1892).

writers have never had a monopoly on producing children's books about African American life and culture."[261] Below, I examine one book written by a white woman, three books written by African American women, and several stories published in the African American periodical, *The Brownies' Book*. I explore how their heroines align with the idealized femininity entrenched in contemporary American society. The inclusion of the white-authored text provides context, as authors of color closely align their heroines with the cult of domesticity and Christianity, the opposite of the "unfeminine" Black characters white authors typically portray. African American authors' texts imply that demure femininity, as outlined by the cult of domesticity, could be the key for heroines to inspire racial uplift.

6.1 The Cult of Domesticity

There is a range of white-authored fiction featuring African American girls. For example, many of the texts examined in this Element, including Finley's *Elsie Dinsmore* (1867) and Speed's *The Carter Girls* (1917), feature African American girls as minor characters. They are often one-dimensional background characters (typically enslaved or servants) who adhere to African American female stereotypes; these characters rarely align with the cult of domesticity. The most well-known is arguably Harriet Beecher Stowe's Topsy in *Uncle Tom's Cabin* (1852).[262] This book sold 3,000,000 copies before the Civil War, a text "unprecedented in its sale and worldwide popularity."[263] Stowe's novel is not traditionally girls' literature, but Topsy, "a caricature of black girlhood that is informed by racist depictions of black women,"[264] is arguably a touchstone for many white authors' African American characters, in part because of the text's vast popularity.[265] Brigitte Fielder identifies the

---

[261] R. S. Bishop, *Free within Ourselves: The Development of African American Children's Literature* (London: Heinemann, 2007), p. xii.

[262] H. B. Stowe, *Uncle Tom's Cabin* (Boston, MA: Jewett, 1852).

[263] Tebbel, Vol. I, pp. 222, 388.

[264] Fielder, "Black girls, White girls, American girls," p. 325.

[265] The book history of Uncle Tom's Cabin and its legacy are widely researched, cf. Bernstein, *Racial Innocence*; B. Hochman, *Uncle Tom's Cabin and the Reading*

dichotomy between the white and African American girl in Stowe's story, namely, that Stowe "elevat[es] and prioritiz[es]" the "abolitionist white girl" (Little Eva) and has a "caricatured depiction of the enslaved black girl" (Topsy).[266] Only under Little Eva's kindness can Topsy receive love from others and from God, justifying Little Eva's mission, the arguable narrative focus. When Little Eva dies, Topsy serves as her living memorial; thus, even when physically separated from her white savior, Topsy's humanity relies on her connection to her. Like many nineteenth-century African American characters written by white authors, Topsy never assumes an angelic femininity.

In what might be read as a direct response to white authors' characterization, African American female authors' heroines developed into an idealized feminine role. Nazera Sadiq Wright notes that African American girls were used as "tools to put forward their social and political agendas," and, as such, "[African American] writers relied on black girls as emblems of home and family."[267] This section examines two books by the African American author, Amelia E. Johnson. Each features a heroine who assumes her place as a quiet, Christian woman and cares for a home. Johnson wrote both *Clarence and Corinne; or, God's Way* (1890)[268] and *The Hazeley Family* (1894)[269] for the American Baptist Publication Society; the latter is widely considered the first African American children's novel.[270] Both novels are

Revolution: Race Literacy, Childhood, and Fiction, 1851–1911 (Amherst: University of Massachusetts Press, 2011).

[266] Fielder, "Black girls, White girls, American girls," p. 329.

[267] N. S. Wright, *Black Girlhood in the Nineteenth Century* (Urbana, IL: University of Illinois Press, 2016), p. 2.

[268] A. E. Johnson, *Clarence and Corinne; or, God's Way* (Oxford: Oxford University Press, 1988; original 1890).

[269] A. E. Johnson, *The Hazeley Family* (Oxford: Oxford University Press, 1988; original 1894).

[270] L. D'Amico, "Finding God's way: Amelia E. Johnson's *Clarence and Corinne* as a path to religious resistance for African American children" in A. M. Duane and K. Capshaw, eds., *Who Writes for Black Children? African American Children's Literature before 1900* (Minneapolis: University of Minnesota Press, 2017), pp. 182–99, p. 182.

distinctly Christian, following earlier girls' literature traditions, such as Finley's *Elsie Dinsmore*. In being religious, the femininity they promote is socially conservative, closely following the cult of domesticity.

Significantly, Johnson's characters are "racially ambiguous." According to some critics, the lack of racial markings means the characters are interpreted as white,[271] and indeed the illustrations in both novels (see Figure 20) feature characters whose skin is not shaded in, neither do they have the stereotyped, exaggerated facial features often given to African American characters at this time. Jennifer Harris reads Johnson's characters as racially complex, noting that "her racially unmarked characters might speak not to a desire to obscure race"[272] but an opportunity to read one's own race in the characters. Notably, "African American and black Canadian readers might, knowing Johnson's own race, read the characters as black."[273] The racial ambiguity is most likely the result of the predominantly white publishing house, so I read these characters as African American, with the acknowledgement that this interpretation is not universally accepted.

These books have also been critiqued for not dealing with African American social issues of the day, such as lynching and Jim Crow laws.[274] Their absence is true of nineteenth-century children's literature generally, which rarely discusses lynching and is more likely to include the Jim Crow caricature than the namesake laws. Arguably, Johnson's texts subtly address these social issues. In the nineteenth century, there was an emphasis on African American women saving their families, and therefore their race, by leading them spiritually. If they could create a home of love and Christian morals, then their families would rise to the middle class.[275] The woman as spiritual guide is central to much of the sentimental women's

---

[271] H. Spillers, "Introduction" in *Clarence and Corinne; or, God's Way* (Oxford: Oxford University Press, 1988), p. xxvii.

[272] J. Harris, "Black Canadian contexts: The case of Amelia E. Johnson," *African American Review*, 49.3 (2016), 241–59, p. 249.

[273] Ibid.   [274] Spillers, "Introduction," p. xxvii.

[275] B. Christian, "Introduction" in *The Hazeley Family* (Oxford: Oxford University Press, 1988), p. xxx.

Figure 20 Amelia Johnson, *The Haʒeley Family* (Pennsylvania, 1894), frontispiece – Project Gutenberg

fiction of the nineteenth century,[276] making its use in African American girls' fiction a further unifying factor between the previously explored women's fiction and girls' literature.

Clarence and Corinne follows a brother and sister dual protagonist through their childhood into adulthood. The two siblings most likely live in the north, far away from plantations. Nevertheless, their initial home life is far from idyllic: their father is an alcoholic, and their mother is ineffective. When their mother dies, their father leaves, and the two children are separated. With overt Christian themes, there are parallels between Corinne and Elsie Dinsmore, in spite of their racial and class differences. Corinne is a meek girl, "different" from her family members: "nervous; such a tender little plant!"[277] When exposed to cruelty, Corinne falls ill, unable to defend herself; similarly, a meek Elsie lives with unkind relatives. For Elsie and Corinne, these difficulties lead them to Christianity, and both texts justify this suffering as God's will. This reasoning aligns with the angel-of-the-house ideology, which glorifies "women's passive suffering"[278] as part of Christian femininity, not to encourage change, but to demonstrate their angelic natures, which is true for Corinne and Elsie.

Both heroines require parental love to fully strengthen them; faith alone is not sufficient to dispel their nervousness. Elsie's confidence stems from her restored relationship with her father. Corinne eventually gains foster parents who nurture her growth into a Christian woman. As an adult, Corinne is her foster parents' "sunbeam":[279] Corinne develops into a selfless, caring woman, befitting the cult of domesticity. While this demure femininity may not appear radical to modern eyes, the close association between Corinne's story and the once-popular Elsie, offers some semblance of equality for African American heroines. Within the context of her class and race, Corinne follows patterns set before her by Elsie and heroines like her, and eventually lays claim to a similar womanhood: a home and marriage of her own.

Much like Johnson's Corinne, Flora Hazeley in *The Hazeley Family* is similarly angelic throughout Johnson's novel. Very little growth happens

---

[276] Baym, *Woman's Fiction*, p. 44. [277] Johnson, *Clarence and Corinne*, p. 19.
[278] Noble, *Masochistic Pleasure*, p. 47. [279] Johnson, *Clarence and Corinne*, p. 182.

for her character; the narrator observes: "Flora was no longer a girl, but a well-grown young woman – changed and yet not changed. She had matured with years; but it was easy to discern the same merry, thoughtful Flora of old days."[280] "Merry" is not typical of idealized femininity, but Flora's merriness is more of a cheerfulness that underscores Flora's actions. Flora's mother does not embody the cult of domesticity, as she does not possess "particularly affectionate or mother feeling toward [Flora],"[281] neither is the family religious. When Flora meets Ruth, a Christian girl who deftly manages her own household, Flora is inspired to transform her home and family. As a result, in large part due to Flora's efforts, Flora's brothers stay home and give up their vices. Her family also begins attending church. Flora's ability to save not only her mother, but also her brothers, aligns with the "redemptive role" assigned to American girlhood generally, in particular, "the duty of a sister to make home so pleasant for young men that they would not be tempted to look elsewhere for diversion."[282] By the novel's end, Flora is rewarded with an inheritance.

Significantly, Flora does not marry, neither does the novel allude to her marriage. In reforming her home life, Flora has in many ways grown down. In spite of her capabilities as a housekeeper, a mother figure to her brothers, and perfect daughter to her mother, she never steps into the roles of actual wife and mother. The novel ends with a marriage: Flora's brother marries her childhood friend, Lottie. Flora remains at the home she inherited with few responsibilities, "flitt[ing] about happy and contented."[283] This outcome is virtually unheard of in girls' literature, making this novel an important milestone for the whole genre. Flora assumes a carefree life, escaping the intersectional restrictions that accompany being an African American wife and mother in the late nineteenth century, as race and poverty often demanded more work from African American women. Johnson's two novels present a conservative femininity for its heroines, but Flora, to an extent, defines her relationship to the cult of domesticity.

---

[280] Ibid., p. 171.   [281] Ibid., p. 17.   [282] Welter, *Dimity Convictions*, p. 5.
[283] Johnson, *Hazeley Family*, p. 171.

6.2 A Reimagined Femininity

Although published before *The Hazeley Family*, Harper's 1888 novel *Trial and Triumph*[284] takes Flora's nonmarital ending a step further, providing her heroine with a career that moves the efforts of the cult of domesticity away from the home (and its supposed influence on society) and directly into the community. *Trial and Triumph* was originally serialized in the African American magazine, *The Christian Reporter*. Unlike Johnson's novels, *Trial and Triumph* is explicitly intended for African American readers, and the subjects broached in this novel, such as racial prejudice, emphasize that intention. Similarly, the novel has a dual readership of children and adults, making it an outlier in the girls' literature genre. Throughout the novel characters discuss how to navigate a society in which they are not treated as equals. For example, at her integrated school, Annette is taunted for having black skin, leading to a discussion with Annette's mother figure about race. Annette is reminded to be proud of her skin color: "In this country, Annette, color has been made a sore place; it has been associated with slavery, poverty and ignorance. You cannot change your color, but you can try to change the association connected with our complexions."[285] These inclusions make the lack of racial identification more apparent in Johnson's works and pave the way for some of the racial pride pieces featured in *The Brownies' Book*.

Harper's novel centers around Annette's coming of age. Her character serves as almost a standin for the African American community. Much like Johnson's Corinne and Clarence, Annette is an orphan. Annette's lack of a father's love and support is considered one of Annette's many disadvantages. Annette is raised by her grandmother, Mrs. Harcourt. While Mrs. Harcourt does not necessarily understand Annette's sensitivity and love of poetry, she sacrifices to give Annette an education. Annette's other-mother is Mrs. Lasette, a former teacher who embodies the cult of domesticity. Mrs. Lasette represents the belief that the betterment of the African

---

[284] F. E. W. Harper, *Minnie's Sacrifice; Sowing and Reaping; Trial and Triumph: Three Rediscovered Novels by Frances E.W. Harper* (Boston, MA: Beacon Press, 1994).

[285] Ibid., pp. 219–20.

American community begins with mothers: "the moment the crown of motherhood fell upon her, . . . she had poured a new interest into the welfare of her race."[286] As a result of Mrs. Lasette's influence, Annette's commencement speech, "Mission of the Negro," aligns with Mrs. Lasette's charitable focus.[287] Annette follows Mrs. Lasette's pursuit, but rather than helping the community as a mother and wife, Annette assumes a more direct role.

Of the heroines examined in this Element, Annette arguably has the most agency. Annette is aware of "the social contempt which society has heaped upon the colored people"; rather than demurring at such contempt, she is a "fiery, impetuous and impulsive girl, and her school experience [brings] it out."[288] In receiving her education, something not readily available to nineteenth-century African American girls, Annette learns to resist the role society offers and becomes a teacher. Annette's home is described as "a beautiful place of fragrance and flowers."[289] The imagery is associated with fertility, asserting her connection to a femininity apart from the domestic parlor. Her ability to tame one woman's "wild" son shows her mothering capabilities. At the novel's end, Annette's former fiancé arrives, offering marriage: "He had come not to separate her from her cherished life work, but to help her in uplifting and helping those among whom her lot was cast as a holy benediction."[290] Now she can be a wife and a community helper, forming a new kind of womanhood in girls' literature. This unique role may exist in part because of *Trial and Triumph*'s dual readership, making its classification as *girls'* literature tenuous at best. Harper's novel serves as a companion piece to Johnson's *The Hazeley Family*, wherein Flora, who has no job, does not need marriage to assure her place as a culturally approved woman.

6.3 The Brownies' Book

African American girls' books were not generally included in mainstream publication from 1850 to 1940. Indeed, as noted in section 1, African American girls' literature comprises only a small percentage of present-day publications. However, as the books chosen in this section demonstrate,

---

[286] Harper, *Trial and Triumph*, p. 185. [287] Ibid., p. 241. [288] Ibid., p. 226.
[289] Ibid., p. 284. [290] Ibid., p. 285.

African American authors found ways for their works to reach child readers. One of the most notable from the early twentieth century is DuBois' *The Brownies' Book*, whose purpose is to meet "the great need which exists for literature adapted to colored children, and indeed to all children who live in a world of varied races."[291] The periodical ran for two years, eventually closing due to a lack of subscriptions.[292] In addition to biographies, advice columns, and fantasy stories, there are realistic stories featuring African American heroines and written by African American women. Although the implied reader of *The Brownies' Book* was African American children of both genders and indeed, of all races as noted above, I view these stories as subsets of girls' literature. The subgenres – family, orphan, and school stories – appear as various short stories in *The Brownies' Book*; a few from each subgenre are explored below.

There is a notable lack of didacticism in many of these stories. The family stories explored earlier in the Element, center on white girls who must learn to become angelically feminine, with Jo March following the quintessential trajectory of the family-story heroine. With more than fifty years between *Little Women* and *The Brownies' Book*, we see a marked difference in these family-story heroines. For example, in Pocahontas Foster's "The Chocolate Cake,"[293] Gwendolyn's aunt asks her to visit to teach Gwendolyn so-called feminine skills, such as darning and cooking. Readers familiar with family stories might presume that Gwendolyn will master these skills, bringing her closer to idealized femininity. However, as a result of Gwendolyn's mischievousness, her aunt sends her home. Instead of punishing her, her father asserts: "I don't believe I want you to be a cook any way. I think I'd rather have you study music."[294] Here, cooking is not an essential feminine skill, but a career path. His comment may not be as progressive as modern readers might assume, as African American women often had to earn a living.[295] Still, were Gwendolyn to run her own

---

[291] W.E. B. DuBois' and Dill, "Valedictory," *The Brownies' Book*, 2.12 (1921), p. 354.

[292] Ibid.

[293] P. Foster, "The Chocolate Cake," *The Brownies' Book*, 2.4 (1921), pp. 116–20.

[294] Ibid., p. 120.   [295] Wright, *Black Girlhood*, p. 3.

household, presumably she would need to cook for her family, which is overlooked. Similarly, in Lillian A. Turner's "How Lilimay 'Kilt' the Chicken,"[296] Lilimay misunderstands a family friend's request and kills a chicken. Whereas Marjorie's misunderstandings have consequences in *Marjorie's Vacation*, there is no lesson for Lilimay. Both *Brownies'* stories feature heroines away from home and their somewhat idealized mothers.

An example of didacticism in girls' family stories occurs when a mother is present. In Maud Wilcox Niedermeyer's "The Pink Banana,"[297] Esther learns a lesson about money and greed. Her mother advises her to spend wisely, but instead, Esther buys and eats sweets. When Esther becomes ill, she resolves to listen to her mother's advice in the future. Esther's mother resembles Marmee from *Little Women*, giving her daughter space in which to make mistakes. Esther is perhaps on the trajectory to the more idealized femininity that her mother embodies.

In several of the girls' orphan stories, there emerges a sense of duty to family. Overall, these stories do not feature orphans who change those around them, only orphans who themselves change.[298] In Augusta E. Bird's "Impossible Kathleen,"[299] the eponymous protagonist must leave college and live with her father and half-siblings. There she assumes housekeeping duties and begins teaching local African American children. Kathleen realizes that her "mission" is not to have a "grand career" but to help this community.[300] Like the orphaned Jane in *Jane Allen of the Sub-Team*, Kathleen speaks aloud to her dead mother, aligning her decision with her mother's decision years ago and thereby, aligning herself with an idealized

---

[296] Lillian A. Turner, "How Lilimay 'Kilt' the Chicken," *The Brownies' Book*, 2.9 (1921), pp. 251–2.

[297] Maud Wilcox Niedermeyer, "The Pink Banana," *The Brownies' Book*, 2.10 (1921), pp. 299–300.

[298] Patsy's adoption in Grace White's "Not Wanted" is an exception. The woman's decision to adopt was ostensibly influenced by Patsy. In G. White, "Not wanted," *The Brownies' Book*, 1.4 (1920), pp. 115–16.

[299] A. E. Bird, "Impossible Kathleen," *The Brownies' Book*, 1.10 (1920), pp. 297–303.

[300] Ibid., p. 303.

femininity. While Kathleen's mother's decision led to marriage and a family, we might see Kathleen's position as teacher for these children as a family unit of its own. There is a progression from helping her half-siblings to helping the community, and, in doing so, she is lifting up her race, much as Annette in *Trial and Triumph* does.

Ella T. Madden's "A Girl's Will,"[301] tells a similar story of Helen La Rose who sacrifices college for her family. Notably, in both stories, gender does not prevent a girl from attending college. Indeed, Helen plans to work her way through college like Booker T. Washington. When her friend observes Washington is male, Helen responds that she is "as smart as any boy. Dad said so ... I can do anything I want to, if I want to hard enough."[302] In this way, Helen and her father attempt to erase gender differences. However, when Helen's mother dies unexpectedly, "Helen took her mother's place in the household."[303] Not until her younger siblings grow up can now thirty-five-year-old Helen attend college. These burdens fall to Helen as the eldest, but also, presumably, because she is a girl. The purported gender equality is quickly superseded by her siblings' need for a mother figure. Unlike Kathleen, Helen does not have to give up higher education; Helen's responsibility is time-bound. African American orphan heroines may have a duty beyond themselves: for Kathleen, that duty becomes an inner mission, and, for Helen, that duty does not stop her from eventually following her dream.

Whereas the school stories in section 5 often focus on the social aspects outside the classroom, these African American school stories focus on succeeding within the classroom. Unlike the novels in that section, these stories feature younger protagonists who live at home, which might account for some of the difference. The variance might also be one of race. Elizabeth Schafer notes: "Scholastic success and failure is a prevalent theme in African American children's literature."[304] In Willie Mae King's "Why Bennie was

---

[301] E. T. Madden's "A girl's will," *The Brownies' Book*, 1.2 (1920), pp. 54–6.

[302] Ibid., p. 54.   [303] Ibid.

[304] E. Schafer, "'I'm gonna glory in learnin': Academic aspirations of African American characters in children's literature," *African American Review*, 32.1 (1998), pp. 57–66, p. 57.

Fired,"[305] eleven-year-old Bennie loses her job when practicing for a school contest makes her late for work. When she wins first prize, she realizes that her prize money is more than she could have made working in a month. Bennie does not resume working but instead, takes the vacation her teacher offers her. Her story's moral is that education is more valuable than working.

A similar pride in education occurs in Ethel M. Caution's "Polly Sits Tight."[306] Polly is poor but the smartest student in her class. Because she does not want her classmates to see her shoes, Polly refuses to participate. Then Polly remembers her now-dead father's advice and proudly goes to the board, deciding to live up to the faith others have in her. Notably, the narrator makes a point of noting that Polly has faith in herself, making academic success personal for the heroine and, presumably, the reader. Polly's fears are not realized, because instead of shoes, her classmates see "a black girl with beaming face, mouth tightly shut, head held high, go to the board and quietly, but quickly and thoroughly demonstrate the solution of the problem that had baffled them all."[307] Investing in education becomes overtly didactic in Blanche Lynn Patterson's "The Heritage."[308] When Julie resolves to quit school, an older African American woman sympathizes, but urges Julie to remember her heritage. She tells Julie: "The only reward that yo'r unhappy fo'fathers ever will get is through you, an' if you fail, you disappoint yo'r whole race."[309] This thought lifts Julie's spirits as she feels supported by her ancestors who look to her success. "The Heritage" gives voice to the implied theme in the other stories: African American children have opportunities not afforded to many of their relatives, and thus, they have the responsibility to pursue them.

Although not always as explicit, the emphasis on racial uplift from *Trial and Triumph* echoes in these stories. The readers of *The Brownies'*

---

[305] Willie Mae King, "Why Bennie was fired," *The Brownies' Book*, 1.7 (1920), pp. 222–4.

[306] E. M. Caution, "Polly Sits Tight," *The Brownies' Book*, 2.11 (1921), p. 308.

[307] Ibid.

[308] B. L. Patterson, "The Heritage," *The Brownies' Book*, 1.8 (1920), pp. 249–50.

[309] Ibid., p. 250.

Book represent the next generation of African American children, and, in these stories, we see duty comes first, dreams can still be pursued, and education is central to success. The cult of domesticity that was reimagined for *Trial and Triumph* and *The Hazeley Family* is reimagined here too. Some of the stories feature heroines learning lessons, but the end trajectory is not necessarily to be a wife and mother, or even to "grow down." The older heroines do not have husbands or even beaux; instead, heroines might pursue a career in music or attend college at the age of thirty-five. The reason might be in part the presumably younger implied audience of the periodical, although this theme seems to be the natural next step from the earlier novels.

Early African American girls' literature, as written by African American women authors, features a femininity that aligns with the cult of domesticity insofar as its views on a woman's potential to uplift those around her. Their publication often occurred in African American periodicals, showing agency in the African American publishing community to share these messages. While these texts align with the conviction that community revitalization begins with mothers, some heroines directly engage with and affect change in their communities. As Wright notes, African American girls "were considered more likely to carry out the aspirations and promises of racial progress."[310] Therefore, they seek broader societal acceptance, and, as a result, these heroines work harder than their white counterparts. In addition to growing down, they have to navigate racism and racial uplift in their attempts to assimilate. These heroines separate African American girlhood from the caricatures written by many white authors, proving that African American girls can conform to the standards of the day and make concerted efforts to bring love and hope to their community.

[310] Wright, *Black Girlhood*, p. 3.

7 Conclusion

Over the course of this Element, the thread of girls' literature becomes clear. With its roots in early American women's literature, we see that American girls' literature continues the *bildungsroman* of girls heading towards marriage and motherhood, towards the cult of domesticity. Whether the girls receive an education, have a mother, or were orphaned, whether they are white or African American, they are expected to marry. If they do not marry, they are often the exception among other happily married girls in their story. The books published and marketed to girls for almost 100 years, beginning with Warner's *The Wide, Wide World* in 1850 and ending with Sawyer's *The Year of Jubilo* in 1940, show girls learning to become selfless and subservient, in order to perform prescribed femininity. With very few exceptions, girls are depicted embracing the role society laid out for them. As a result, American girls' literature, as demonstrated in the previous sections, shows a very narrow picture of girlhood.

Furthermore, this fictionalized womanhood was skewed to privilege certain backgrounds and experiences. The female characters featured in the earlier sections are generally white, middle class, Protestant, able-bodied, cis-gendered, and heterosexual. None is an immigrant, or identified with a culture other than the English-speaking, Caucasian understanding of American. This type of girlhood is not representative of American girlhood, either at the turn of the century or today. There are silences or caricatures in place of a reflection of reality. While the African American girls' literature examined in section 6 begins to address this lack of diversity, it is clear that these few early novels only begin to expand the generic definition. Although these novels, particularly those written by African American writers, feature racial pride, the womanhood they are asked to enter still aligns with the restrictive cult of domesticity.

This Element is, of course, one of numerous attempts to call attention to the need of diversity in children's literature. Movements like We Need Diverse Books and #1000BlackGirlBooks bring awareness to and work to increase the lack of voices in children's publishing. Scholarship, like the 2017 edited collection, *Who Writes for Black Children? African American*

Children's Literature before 1900,[311] begins to locate literature that was lost. As we prioritize the uncovering and production of diverse voices, then we must revisit how the genre of girls' literature is defined, both historically and contemporaneously.

As we examine the multitude of published girls' books, we expand what girls' literature has been and what girls' literature can be. The natural next step is then to ask what girls' literature is today. What subgenres comprise it? What is the underpinning *bildungsroman*? Are we still asking girls to enter heterosexual marriages to fulfill their feminine duty, or have we problematized this expectation? The answers to these questions allow us to understand the potential of girls' literature as a reflection of American society, as well as its influence on young readers.

Modern readers of the girls' literature explored in this Element often label its *bildungsroman* repressive, even anti-feminist. In the twenty-first century, many readers like to believe that girls both in fiction and real life are able to aspire to more than heterosexual marriage and motherhood. Yet, this long arm of tradition sometimes seems inescapable. In Suzanne Collins' dystopian *The Hunger Games* trilogy (2008–10),[312] the heroine Katniss Everdeen questions her role as symbol for the rebellion, pushing against society's objectification of her. She does not exhibit traditional feminine qualities, such as care towards and sacrifice for others (apart from a select few people), but once a stable government is established, her feminine capabilities appear restored. Katniss reluctantly becomes a wife and mother, stepping into a quiet *domestic* life, where "[o]nly the joy of holding [my daughter] in my arms could tame [my fear of the future]."[313] This series, featuring a nuanced female character, capitulates to the nineteenth-century *bildungsroman*. Female characters with choice and agency are not always as easy to locate as we might presume.

---

[311] A. M. Duane and K. Capshaw, eds., *Who Writes for Black Children? African American Children's Literature before 1900* (Minneapolis: University of Minnesota Press, 2017).

[312] S. Collins, *The Hunger Games* series(New York: Scholastic, 2008–10).

[313] S. Collins, *Mockingjay* (New York: Scholastic, 2010), p. 389.

My hope in defining the book history of girls' literature is to help give writers, publishers, and academics a way forward. Classifying girls' literature in its earliest forms helps us establish a new girls' literature, something to push against as we form an inclusive look at fictionalized girlhood as it exists in the nineteenth and twentieth centuries and contemporaneously: to define a girls' literature that ventures beyond the single-story *bildungsroman* ending of marriage and motherhood, that includes the multitude of girls' identities, and thus, to locate a genre that actually reflects American girlhood.

Bibliography

Primary Texts

Alcott, L. M. (1868–9). *Little Women*. Boston, MA: Roberts Brothers.

Bancroft, E. (1917). *Jane Allen of the Sub-Team*. Akron, OH: Saalfield Publishing.

Blanchard, A. E. (1906). *The Four Corners*. Philadelphia: G.W. Jacobs.

Blume, J. (1975). *Forever*. New York: Bradbury Press.

Brown, H. D. (1886). *Two College Girls*. Boston, MA: Houghton, Mifflin.

Bunyan, J. (1678). *Pilgrim's Progress*. London: Nathaniel Ponder.

Canfield, D. (1916). *Understood Betsy*. New York: Henry Holt.

Champney, L. W. (1883). *Three Vassar Girls Abroad: Rambles of Three College Girls on a Vacation Trip through France and Spain for Amusement and Instruction*. Boston, MA: Estes and Lauriat.

Champney, L. W. (1885). *Three Vassar Girls in South America. A Holiday Trip of Three College Girls through the Southern Continent, Up the Amazon, Down the Madeira, Across the Andes, and Up the Pacific Coast to Panama*. Boston, MA: Estes and Lauriat.

Collins, S. (2008–10). *The Hunger Games* series. New York: Scholastic.

Collins, S. (2010). *Mockingjay*. New York: Scholastic.

Coolidge, S. (1872). *What Katy Did*. Boston, MA: Robert Brothers.

Fauset, J. R., ed., (1920–1). *The Brownies' Book*. New York: DuBois and Dill.

Finley, M. (1867–1905). *Elsie Dinsmore series*. New York: M.W. Dodd.

Finley, M. (1867). *Elsie Dinsmore*. New York: M.W. Dodd.

Finley, M. (1868). *Elsie's Holidays at Roselands*. New York: M.W. Dodd.

Follen, E. L. C. (1838). *Sketches of Married Life*. Boston, MA: Hilliard, Gray, and Co.

Gilman, C. (1838). *Recollections of a Southern Matron*. New York: Harper & Brothers.

Graves, A. J. (1844). *Girlhood and Womanhood; or, Sketches of my Schoolmates*. Boston, MA: T.H. Carter.

Grove, H. P. (1931). *Betty Lee* series. New York: A.L. Burt.

Harper, F. E. W. (1892/2010). *Iola Leroy, or Shadows Uplifted*. New York: Penguin Classics.

Harper, F. E. W. (1888/1994). *Minnie's Sacrifice; Sowing and Reaping; Trial and Triumph: Three Rediscovered Novels by Frances E.W. Harper*. Boston, MA: Beacon Press.

Johnson, A. E. (1890/1988). *Clarence and Corinne; or, God's Way*. Oxford: Oxford University Press.

Johnson, A. E. (1894/1988). *The Hazeley Family*. Oxford: Oxford University Press.

Johnston, A. F. (1895–1907). *Little Colonel* series. Boston, MA: L.C. Page.

Johnston, A. F. (1895). *Little Colonel*. Boston, MA: L.C. Page.

Johnston, A. F. (1903). *The Little Colonel at Boarding-School*. Boston, MA: L.C. Page.

Johnston, A. F. (1907). *The Little Colonel's Knight Comes Riding*. Boston, MA: L.C. Page.

Lester, P. (1922). *Marjorie Dean, College Freshman*. New York: A.L. Burt.

Lester, P. (1917–25). *Marjorie Dean* series. New York: A.L. Burt.

Lovelace, M. H. (1940–55). *Betsy-Tacy* series. New York: Thomas Y. Crowell.

Lovelace, M. H. (1946). *Betsy in Spite of Herself*. New York: Thomas Y. Crowell.

Pascal, F. (1983–2003). *Sweet Valley High* series. New York: Random House.

Patmore, C. (1854). *The Angel in the House*. London: John W. Parker.

Porter, E. (1913). *Pollyanna*. Boston, MA: L.C. Page.

Porter, E. (1915). *Pollyanna Grows Up*. Boston, MA: L.C. Page.

Richards, L. H. (1921–3). *Caroline* series. Boston, MA: Little, Brown.

Richards, L. H. (1921). *Then Came Caroline.*Boston, MA: Little, Brown.

Rowson, S. (1794). *Charlotte Temple*. Philadelphia: Matthew Carey.

Sawyer, R. (1936). *Roller Skates*. New York: Viking Press.

Sawyer, R. (1940). *The Year of Jubilo*. New York: Viking Press.

Sedgwick, C. M. (1822). *A New-England Tale*. New York: Bliss & White.

Speed, N. (1917). *The Carter Girls*. New York: A.L. Burt.

Stowe, H. B. (1852). *Uncle Tom's Cabin*. Boston, MA: John P. Jewett.

Stratton Porter, G. (1909). *A Girl of the Limberlost*. New York: Doubleday, Page.

Warde, M. (1906). *Betty Wales, Freshman*. Philadelphia: Penn Publishing.

Warde, M. (1912). *Nancy Lee*. Philadelphia: Penn Publishing.

Warner, S. (1850). *The Wide, Wide World*. New York: G.P. Putnam.

Webster, J. (1903). *When Patty Went to College*. New York: The Century Company.

Webster, J. (1911). *Just Patty*. New York: The Century Company.

Webster, J. (1912). *Daddy Long Legs*. New York: The Century Company.

Webster, J. (1915). *Dear Enemy*. New York: The Century Company.

Wells, C. (1907). *Marjorie's Vacation*. New York: Dodd, Mead.

Wiggin, K. D. (1903). *Rebecca of Sunnybrook Farm*. Boston, MA: Houghton, Mifflin.

Wilder, L. I. (1932–71). *Little House* series. New York: Harper & Brothers.

Secondary Texts

Abate, M. A. (2008). *Tomboys: A Literary and Cultural History*. Philadelphia: Temple University Press.

Advertisement 151. (1910). *The Bookman: A Review of Books and Life*, 30(6), 822.

Advertisement 13. (1918). *The Youth's Companion*, 92(42), 544.

Avery, G. (1992). Home and family: English and American ideals in the nineteenth century. In D. Butts, ed., *Stories and Society: Children's*

Literature in its Social Context. Basingstoke: Macmillan Academic and Professional, pp. 37–49.

Avery, G. (1994). *Behold the Child: American Children and their Books 1621–1922*. London: Bodley Head.

Baym, N. (1992). *Feminism and American Literary History*. New Brunswick, NJ: Rutgers University Press.

Baym, N. (1993). *Woman's Fiction: A Guide to Novels by and about Women in America, 1820–1870*, 2nd edn. Ithaca, New York: Cornell University Press.

Bernstein, R. (2011). *Racial Innocence: Performing American Childhood from Slavery to Civil Rights*. New York: New York University Press.

Bishop, R. S. (2007). *Free within Ourselves: The Development of African American Children's Literature*. Portsmouth, NH: Heinemann.

Butler, J. (1990). *Gender Trouble*. New York: Routledge.

Christian, B. (1988).Introduction. In *The Hazeley Family*. Oxford: Oxford University Press, pp. xxvii–xxxvii.

Cockett, L. S. & Kleinberg, J. R. (1994). Periodical literature for African-American young adults: A neglected resource. In K. P. Smith, ed., *African-American Voices in Young Adult Literature: Tradition, Transition, Transformation*. Latham, MD: Scarecrow Press, pp. 115–67.

Cooperative Children's Book Center. (2020). Books by and/or about Black, Indigenous, and People of Color. https://ccbc.education.wisc.edu/litera ture-resources/ccbc-diversity-statistics/books-by-and-or-about-poc -2019/.

D'Amico, L. (2017). Finding God's way: Amelia E. Johnson's *Clarence and Corinne* as a path to religious resistance for African American children. In A. M. Duane & K. Capshaw, eds., *Who Writes for Black Children? African American Children's Literature before 1900*. Minneapolis: University of Minnesota Press, pp. 182–99.

Dorré, G. M. (2006). *Victorian Fiction and the Cult of the Horse*. Abingdon: Ashgate.

Douglas, A. (1977). *The Feminization of American Culture*. New York: Alfred A. Knopf.

Duane, A. M. & Capshaw, K., eds. (2017). *Who Writes for Black Children? African American Children's Literature before 1900*. Minneapolis: University of Minnesota Press.

Fielder, B. (2017). Black girls, white girls, American girls: Slavery and racialized perspectives in abolitionist and neoabolitionist children's literature. *Tulsa Studies in Women's Literature*, 36(2), 323–52.

Foster, S. & Simons, J. (1995). *What Katy Read: Feminist Re-Readings of "Classic" Stories for Girls*. Iowa City: University of Iowa Press.

Fraustino, L. R. & Coats, K. (2016). Mothers wanted. In L. R. Fraustino & K. Coats, eds., *Mothers in Children's and Young Adult Literature: From Eighteenth Century to Postfeminism*. Jackson, MS: University of Mississippi Press, pp. 3–24.

Friedan, B. (1963). *The Feminine Mystique*. New York: W.W. Norton.

Gilbert, S. & Gubar, S. (2000). *The Madwoman in the Attic: The Woman Writer and the Nineteenth-Century Literary Imagination*, 2nd edn. New Haven, CT: Yale University Press.

A girl's bookshelf. (13 Nov. 1921). *New York Times*, BRM9.

Gulliver, L. (1960). *Louisa May Alcott: A Bibliography*. New York: Burt Franklin.

Hale, E. (2010). Disability and the individual talent: Adolescent girlhood in *The Pillars of the House* and *What Katy Did*. *Women's Writing*, 17(2), 343–60.

Harris, J. (2016). Black Canadian contexts: The case of Amelia E. Johnson. *African American Review*, 49(3), 241–59.

Hochman, B. (2011). *Uncle Tom's Cabin and the Reading Revolution: Race Literacy, Childhood, and Fiction, 1851–1911*. Amherst, MA: University of Massachusetts Press.

Inness, S. A. (1995). *Intimate Communities: Representation and Social Transformation in Women's College Fiction, 1895–1910*. Bowling Green, OH: Bowling Green State University Popular Press.

Johnson, D. (1990). *Telling Tales: The Pedagogy and Promise of African American Literature for Youth*. Westport, CT: Greenwood Press.

Keith, L. (2001). *Take Up Thy Bed and Walk: Death, Disability and Cure in Classic Fiction for Girls*. London: Women's Press.

Lubovich, M. (2008). "Married or single?": Catharine Maria Sedgwick on old maids, wives, and marriage. *Legacy*, 25(1), 23–40.

MacLeod, A. S. (1994). *American Childhood: Essays on Children's Literature of the Nineteenth and Twentieth Centuries*. Athens, GA: University of Georgia Press.

Marchalonis, S. (1995). *College Girls: A Century in Fiction*. New Brunswick, NJ: Rutgers University Press.

Matthews, G. (1987). *"Just a Housewife": The Rise and Fall of Domesticity in America*. Oxford: Oxford University Press.

McCandless, A. T. (1987). Concepts of patriarchy in the popular novels of antebellum southern women. *Studies in Popular Culture*, 10(2), 1–16.

Mills, C. (1987). Children in search of a family: Orphan novels through the century. *Children's Literature in Education*, 18(4), 227–39.

Monthly literary bulletin. (1844). *The United States Magazine, and Democratic Review*, 14(71), 552.

Nelson, C. (1991). What Katy read: Susan Coolidge and the image of the Victorian child. In *Children's Literature Quarterly*, 1991 Proceedings, pp. 217–22.

Nikolajeva, M. (2000). *From Mythic to Linear: Time in Children's Literature*. Latham, MD: Scarecrow Press.

Nikolajeva, M. (2005). *Aesthetic Approaches to Children's Literature: An Introduction*. Latham, MD: Scarecrow Press.

Noble, M. (2000). *Masochistic Pleasures of Sentimental Literature*. Princeton, NJ: Princeton University Press.

Oxford English Dictionary Online. (2020). Oxford: Oxford University Press.

Pfeiffer, J. (2016). The romance of othermothering in *Backfisch* books. In L. R. Fraustino & K. Coats, eds., *Mothers in Children's and Young Adult Literature: From Eighteenth Century to Postfeminism*. Jackson, MS: University of Mississippi Press, pp. 59–74.

Pratt, A. (1981). *Archetypal Patterns in Women's Fiction*. Bloomington: Indiana University Press.

Radway, J. A. (1997). *A Feeling for Books: The Book-of-the-Month Club, Literary Taste, and Middle-Class Desire*. Chapel Hill: University of North Carolina Press.

Ravenel, H. E. (1898). *Ravenel Records*. Atlanta, GA: Franklin Printing and Publishing.

Real books for real girls. (Dec. 5, 1909). *New York Times*, LS20.

Review 7. (1898). *The Bookman; a Review of Books and Life*, 7(3), 255.

Rosoff, N. G. & Spencer, S. (2019). *British and American School Stories, 1910–1960: Fiction, Femininity, and Friendship*. Cham, Switzerland: Palgrave Macmillan.

Rowbotham, J. (1989). *Good Girls Make Good Wives: Guidance for Girls in Victorian Fiction*. Oxford: Blackwell Publishing.

Sanders, J. S. (2011). *Disciplining Girls: Understanding the Origins of the Classic Orphan Girl Story*. Baltimore, MD: Johns Hopkins University Press.

Sardella-Ayres, D. (2018). Food and community in American college girl fiction. *FEAST Journal: Consuming Children*, 1, n.p.

Sardella-Ayres, D. (2019). Rewriting and re-whiting *The Little Colonel*: Racial anxieties, tomboyism, and Lloyd Sherman. *Children's Literature*, 47, 79–103.

Sardella-Ayres, D. & Reese, A. N. (2020). Constructing girls' literature through the *bildungsroman* in Canada and the United States. *Girlhood Studies: An Interdisciplinary Journal*, 13(3), 33–49.

Schafer, E. (1998). "I'm gonna glory in learnin'": Academic aspirations of African American characters in children's literature. *African American Review*, 32(1), 57–66.

Seelye, J. (2005).*Jane Eyre's American Daughters: From The Wide, Wide World to Anne of Green Gables a Study of Marginalized Maidens and What They Mean*. Newark: University of Delaware Press.

Showalter, E. (1991). *Sister's Choice: Tradition and Change in American Women's Writing*. Oxford: Oxford University Press.

Showalter, E. (2009). *A Jury of Her Peers: American Woman Writers from Anne Bradstreet to Annie Proulx*. New York: Alfred A. Knopf.

Smedman, M.S. (1985). Martha Finley (26 April 1828–30 January 1909). In G. E. Estes, ed., *American Writers for Children Before 1900*. Detroit, MI: Gale Research, pp. 177–85.

Smith-Rosenberg, C. (1985). *Disorderly Conduct: Visions of Gender in Victorian America*. New York: A.A. Knopf.

Society of Phantom Friends. (1997). *The Girls' Series Companion: 1997*. Henderson, NV: SynSine Press.

Spillers, H. (1988). Introduction. In *Clarence and Corinne; or, God's Way*. Oxford: Oxford University Press, pp. xxvii–xxxviii.

Stoneley, P. (2003). *Consumerism and American Girls' Literature, 1860–1940*. Cambridge: Cambridge University Press.

Tebbel, J. (1972). *The Creation of an Industry, 1630–1865*. Vol. I of *A History of Book Publishing in the United States*. New York: R.R. Bowker.

Tebbel, J. (1975). *The Expansion of an Industry, 1865–1919*. Vol. II of *A History of Book Publishing in the United States*. New York: R.R. Bowker.

Troester, R. R. (1984). Turbulence and tenderness: Mothers, daughters, and "othermothers" in Paule Marshall's *Brown Girl, Brownstones*. *SAGE: A Scholarly Journal on Black Women*, 1(2), 13–16.

Weedon, A. (2019). The uses of quantification. In S. Eliot & J. Rose, eds., *A Companion to the History of the Book*, 2nd ed. Hoboken, NJ: John Wiley & Sons, pp. 31–50.

Welter, B. (1976). *Dimity Convictions: The American Woman in the Nineteenth Century*. Athens: Ohio University Press.

Wright, N. S. (2016). *Black Girlhood in the Nineteenth Century*. Urbana: University of Illinois Press.

Acknowledgments

Thank you to Melanie Griffin, now at the University of Arkansas, and her former colleagues in Special Collections at the University of South Florida Library, as well as to Suzan Alteri and her colleagues at the Baldwin Library of Historical Children's Literature at the University of Florida, for their advice and assistance in locating materials. Thank you also to those at HathiTrust, the Library of Congress, and Project Gutenberg for providing access to works in the public domain. I am indebted to Morag Styles, Maria Nikolajeva, Susan Tan, and Dawn Sardella-Ayres for helping shape my ideas of girls' literature.

Thank you to Eugene Giddens for his work as editor. I am grateful to Peter Cannon for his assistance with the graph and images, as well as his support.

To Peter

Cambridge Elements ☰

Publishing and Book Culture

SERIES EDITOR

Samantha Rayner
University College London

Samantha Rayner is a Reader in UCL's Department of Information Studies. She is also Director of UCL's Centre for Publishing, co-Director of the Bloomsbury CHAPTER (Communication History, Authorship, Publishing, Textual Editing and Reading) and co-editor of the Academic Book of the Future BOOC (Book as Open Online Content) with UCL Press.

ASSOCIATE EDITOR

Leah Tether
University of Bristol

Leah Tether is professor of medieval literature and publishing at the University of Bristol. With an academic background in medieval French and English literature and a professional background in trade publishing, Leah has combined her expertise and developed an international research profile in book and publishing history from manuscript to digital.

About the Series

This series aims to fill the demand for easily accessible, quality texts available for teaching and research in the diverse and dynamic fields of Publishing and Book Culture. Rigorously researched and peer-reviewed Elements will be published under themes, or 'Gatherings'. These Elements should be the first check point for researchers or students working on that area of publishing and book trade history and practice: we hope that, situated so logically at Cambridge University Press, where academic publishing in the UK began, it will develop to create an unrivalled space where these histories and practices can be investigated and preserved.

Cambridge Elements ≡

Publishing and Book Culture

Children's Publishing

Gathering Editor: Eugene Giddens

Eugene Giddens is Skinner-Young Professor of Shakespeare
and Renaissance Literature at Anglia Ruskin University. His
work considers the history of the book from the early modern
period to the present. He is co-author of *Lewis Carroll's* Alice's
Adventures in Wonderland *and* Through the Looking-Glass*:
A Publishing History* (2013).

ELEMENTS IN THE GATHERING

Picture-Book Professors: Academia and Children's Literature
Melissa Terras

Christmas Books for Children
Eugene Giddens

The Rise of American Girls' Literature
Ashley N. Reese

A full series listing is available at: www.cambridge.org/EPBC